S0-AGM-506

SMALL BUSINESS MATTERS

A Collection of Short Essays
on Small Business
and all that Matters

by Tim Fulton

TABLE OF CONTENTS

ABOUT THE AUTHOR

Tim Fulton is a nationally recognized small business consultant and advocate. He has been involved in the field of entrepreneurship for the past thirty years as a successful business owner, a small business counselor, and as an adjunct university professor. In 1994, he started TCF Business Development, an independent management consulting and training practice. During this time he has worked with companies such as Lucent Technologies, Carlson Companies, Insignia ESG, and Georgia Power.

Tim's past work experience also includes serving as the assistant director of the Small Business Development Center at Clayton State University and the director of the Family Business Institute at Florida International University. He has worked with thousands of business start-ups and existing businesses as a catalyst for starting and growing their small business.

Tim's own entrepreneurial experience includes the ownership and operation of several fast-growing retail and service businesses, each of which resulted in a successful exit. In addition, he was one of the founders of a successful Atlanta-based INC 500 internet software company.

Tim currently is a Vistage Group Chair in Atlanta, Georgia. Vistage is an international membership organization for company CEOs and presidents started in 1957. Vistage groups meet monthly and provide a very unique growth experience for their members. Tim works with four Vistage groups with 50+ CEOs and key executives.

Tim Fulton has been published and featured in numerous magazines and newspapers including the *Atlanta Business Chronicle, Entrepreneur Magazine,* and *Catalyst Magazine.* He also publishes his own award-winning electronic monthly newsletter, *Small Business Matters,* for small business owners.

A popular public speaker to both private and public audiences, Tim has spoken to groups from the Association of Small Business Development Centers (ASBDC), the Cruise Line Industry Association (CLIA), and the American Society for Training and Development (ASTD). He has also appeared on television and radio programs as an advocate for small business and entrepreneurship.

Tim earned both his BA and MBA in Economics at Tulane University. In addition, he earned his Certificate in Training and Human Resource Development from Florida International University.

A most sincere thank you to the following people:

Bernie Meineke, Chris Hanks, Josh Rutter,

Steve Reisig, Steve Fader, Cindy Miller,

Barbara Babbit Kaufman, Dave Boivin,

Rafael Pastor, my sons Taylor and Carter, my

mom Dorothy Fulton, and my wife Remy.

Foreword

I have been writing business articles for over twenty years. Most have been for my newsletter *Small Business Matters*. Some have been published in newspapers, magazines, or online. The articles come fairly easily for me as I try to explain basic small business principles using my own experiences and those of my clients. My experience shows that the core principles of running a small business are not difficult. It is the execution of these principles that becomes a challenge. Those darn employees, customers, and government regulators seem to always be getting in the way of a great business strategy.

I hope you enjoy reading these articles. They include insights into my own business experiences, my work with Vistage members, and my family. Many of my best business learning experiences have family origins either with my dad, my wife, or my two sons. At times, I have had to use fictional names to protect the innocent, or myself, but rest assured any small business owner probably could have been my example in many of these stories.

I would like to dedicate this book to my favorite small business operator, my father, Robert Fulton. While he passed away much too early in my entrepreneurial career, the lessons he shared with me in my formative years have been critical to my success. Dad managed Florida's largest wholesale tire distribution business. He was a big man who commanded great respect from his employees and customers. While he instilled a bit of fear in most of his peers, he was also loved by all. He treated everyone fairly and would go out of his way to lend support when needed. He lives with me every day.

Robert Fulton

FOUR WAYS TO PREVENT YOURSELF FROM "ENRONING" YOUR SMALL BUSINESS

March 2002

As a business owner or manager, you've watched the news on Enron the past few months and sat in amazement at how such a company could have made such a mess of itself. Enron has gone from being the Prince of Wall Street to the Court Jester. Free-falling stock prices. Thousands of employees laid off. Retirement accounts insolvent. Chapter 11 bankruptcy. Senate hearings. It's the only news story that could have possibly taken our collective minds off of the 9/11 tragedy and the war in Afghanistan.

As you watched this story unfold, you have considered what a terrible misfortune this has been for the stakeholders in Enron. You have probably also concluded that this type of disaster could never happen to your business. It's not possible that your small business could get "Enroned." Or is it?

The reality is that small businesses meet this same fate far more frequently than we can imagine. The failure rate for small businesses is staggering. Just take a drive down Main Street and look at the empty storefronts. Take a "surf" on the internet and search for those websites you designated as favorites a year ago. How many are still there?

How can you protect your small business from being "Enroned"? Here are four ways:

1. Be *honest* with your company's stakeholders.

According to news reports, top officials at Enron misled their investors, their creditors, and their employees. Employees were even encouraged to continue to invest more of their hard-earned savings into Enron stock after news of the company's demise had begun to appear.

Your employees understand more about your business than you can imagine or you give them credit for. Attempts to mislead them may provide you with short-term gains, but will cripple your company in the long run. Trust your employees with the truth. If the company is in trouble, share those challenges with your employees and enlist their support in facing those challenges.

2. Keep your business *simple.*

Enron took great strides to immensely complicate their business. Offshore deals. Limited partnerships. Creative financing. Their CEO, Kenneth Lay, testified that he was not quite sure what exactly was going on within his own company. Others in senior management positions within the company have offered similar testimony. That's a bad sign.

The most successful small businesses I have witnessed are kept as simple as possible. Simple business proposition. Simple financing strategies. Simple exit strategy. Consider a McDonald's franchise. Operating a McDonald's has been so simplified that an owner can hire a part-time high school student with little or no business experience. Then with minimal training he can then place them at the point of contact with customers and rest assured that his multi-million dollar business investment is in good hands.

3. Carefully *select* and *manage* your external professionals.

These professionals include your accountant, your attorney, your banker, and others. Arthur Andersen is an excellent global accounting firm. They also have an outstanding reputation as management consultants. Enron made the mistake of hiring the firm for both auditing and consulting purposes. These roles inherently conflict and will result in Andersen either going through a name change or being bought by another firm. Enron management should have seen this conflict and used Andersen for one job or the other, but not both.

Small business owners make the same mistakes. They ask their attorneys for answers to accounting questions and their accountants for marketing advice. They allow their bankers to make key strategic management decisions for them. These decisions often result in colossal mistakes. You need these professionals to provide advice and consultation in their areas of expertise. This is important to the stability and growth of your business.

4. Cultivate the *right* corporate culture.

Enron had a culture of rule breaking. Individuals went to great lengths to work around United States tax laws and the Internal Revenue Service. When it became evident last fall that their practices were going to be scrutinized, they ordered massive shredding of important corporate documents. What message did these questionable and possibly illegal actions send to the rest of the Enron employees who witnessed these activities? What ethics were expressed in their actions?

Every company, large and small, has a corporate culture or personality. It can either be crafted or cultivated by senior management or it will take a life of its own based on their actions or lack of actions. It is incumbent upon the business owner or general manager to take responsibility for setting the right example for the employees. Their actions will mirror those of their leaders. If the business owner is cheating and lying to customers, it will only be a matter of time before the employees will assume that is right and proper behavior and so they will do the same.

Enron is not the first and won't be the last global conglomerate to stumble and fall. The key lesson for small businesses is to take notice of the pitfalls that tripped the energy giant and caused it to fall. Enron's pitfalls can just as easily strike and knock down a small business with far less paparazzi and no multi-million dollar bonus for the owner to fall back on.

*"The headline never says,
'Passengers crash airplane.'"*

~ MAURICE MASCARENHAS

LESSONS LEARNED AT THE BALLPARK

May 2002

I often receive my best customer service training in the most unlikely situations.

My 6-year-old son, Taylor, had been pressuring me for weeks to take him to a baseball game. At the time, I was still on strike as a Major League Baseball fan. Hence, I decided to take him to see the local team play in the College Baseball Regional Championships.

The game was terrific. It had all the elements that have made baseball our national pastime: great hitting, exciting fielding, and a late-inning comeback by the home team.

In fact, the home team won the game.

Taylor thoroughly enjoyed the game except for one aspect. He had brought his glove to the game just in case a foul ball happened to drift in our direction. With each pitch, he leaned forward anticipating snagging a souvenir ball.

Unfortunately, not a single ball was hit our way.

After the final out, we weaved our way out of the bleachers toward our car in the parking lot. As we reached the stadium exit, we passed an elderly stadium attendant. He appeared to be either a university alumnus or maybe just a fan of the game that worked the gate to earn a free ticket. As the crowd pushed out onto the street, the old gent stood by the exit gate minding his own business.

As we walked by, the attendant abruptly reached down and grabbed Taylor's glove hand as if my son was concealing contraband in his mitt.

"Son, have you got a baseball in that glove?" he asked suspiciously.

Taylor was startled by the stranger and replied, "No," in a soft whisper.

At that moment, the attendant reached into his pocket, pulled out a baseball and dropped it into Taylor's empty glove.

"Now you do," said the man, smiling broadly. "Come back and see us again."

For a moment, Taylor stood like a statue staring down into his glove in disbelief at his prize. He then looked up at me with a smile that would have melted any father's heart. It brought moisture to my eyes.

I was numb.

Taylor grabbed my arm and tugged me out of the pedestrian traffic to the car. The ball, upon closer examination, was an official game ball that had probably been fouled out of the park and retrieved by the man.

Now, my son knows as much about customer service as I do about the Rugrats. However, he made it perfectly clear that we were going to be regular visitors to that baseball stadium for years to come.

In fact, it's safe to say that he is a baseball fan for life.

In retrospect, I believe that gesture was one of the greatest examples of "knock your socks off" customer service that I've ever witnessed in my life. As a result of a rather inexpensive, but sincere gesture by a stadium attendant, baseball has a lifetime customer. This guy went into my customer service hall of fame.

So what's the moral of this story?

Consider your business or organization. What are your frontline people doing to create lifetime customers? Are they empowered to make marketing decisions, such as the one that stadium attendant made, on the spot?

As much money as we spend on marketing our product or services, we sometimes forget that customers are won and lost on the frontline.

Do you have a Hall of Famer working for you? Or are your customer service representatives shackled by company policies and procedures to the degree that they are unable to capitalize on such "moments of truth?"

See ya at the ballpark.

*"Life is not measured
by the number of breaths we take,
but by the moments
that take our breath away."*

~ JAMES HOLMES

STARTING A SMALL BUSINESS IS JUST LIKE RUNNING THE PEACHTREE ROAD RACE... ONLY TOUGHER

June 2002

I first wrote this article almost twelve years ago after I had completed my first Peachtree Road Race. I was fascinated by the similarities of running the race and starting a small business. I have run the race every year since then. The t-shirts are hanging shrine-like on my basement wall as a testimony to hard work and temporary insanity. I continue to enjoy preparing for, and running each race just as I continue to enjoy helping others grow their respective businesses. Enjoy the article and also please enjoy a happy and safe 4th of July.

I started jogging several years ago. It was a New Year's resolution. Like most of my New Year's resolutions, I was confident that the euphoria of the holiday season would end soon and so would my brief encounter with running. Unfortunately, that was not the case.

Six months into the year, I was still running several times a week and had extended my endurance to about two miles a run. It was at that time that a good friend of mine suggested I enter the Atlanta Peachtree Road Race. What a ludicrous idea! The Peachtree was a 10K or 6.2 mile run. This was way beyond my running capabilities. Besides, there would be 50,000 other runners and several hundred thousand spectators. Not a chance....

As I considered this opportunity, (that's what my friend called it), I realized this would be just about the craziest stunt I had attempted in about fifteen years. That's right. Fifteen years before it was first suggested to me that I manage a family-owned business. In hindsight I had survived that entrepreneurial marathon and two more small businesses after that.

I began to consider the notion that preparing for and participating in this race would be like preparing for and starting a small business. Or would it?

When I decided to enter the Peachtree, the first thing I did was tell my family and close friends of my intentions. This experience reminded me of when I would tell a similar audience about my intentions to start a new business. Most people thought I was crazy, while some people shared the same excitement I did. Some people even offered to help me prepare. However, my wife increased the death benefits on my life insurance policy.

My next step was to initiate some strategic planning. First, I attempted to objectively determine what my condition was at the time. I even did a quick S.W.O.T. (strengths, weaknesses, opportunities, and threats) analysis. I concluded that I was in pretty good physical shape (strength), I had never run anywhere close to six miles before (weakness), the environment of the race should be a motivating factor (opportunity). Hopefully there would be paramedics on call and ready to administer lifesaving techniques (threat).

The second step in strategic planning was to establish several goals. I decided that I wanted to finish the race by my own will, I would not be the last finisher, and I would get an official race t-shirt.

This reminded me of planning for a small business start-up. Most of the time we don't plan to be the biggest or the best company in our industry or market. We tend to only focus on survival. I wonder how I would have placed in the race if I had planned to win. I wonder how successful my businesses would have been if I had planned from the beginning to be the largest, most successful, and most profitable company in the market.

Once I had determined my condition and my destination (my goals), I then had to develop an action plan to facilitate my training. I decided that prior to the race I would run a minimum of three times a week. Every week I would try to push my endurance one step further.

I also needed to conduct a little market research. I needed to study the history of the Peachtree Road Race and the layout of the course. How many spectators would there be? What kind of weather could I expect? Who was my competition? What were past winning times? *(Not particularly relevant in my case.)* What were average times? *(More important.)* What was the worst time last year? *(Critically important.)*

My planning and training took about six months. Coincidentally, the average small business takes six months to start. This is from the time of the initial decision to start the business to the first day of operation. My experience is, that on average, the most successful small businesses are the ones that take the necessary time to plan their business and get "in shape." The businesses that start without a plan of attack and without the necessary resources, then take the quickest exit from the "race."

The day of the Peachtree Road Race finally arrived. I found myself asking the same questions many small business owners ask themselves on their first day of operation: How long will I last? Do I have the resources to finish the race? What if I stumble and fall?

The start of the race reminded me of a business "Grand Opening" with music, drinks, and a lot of paparazzi. Electricity was in the air.

The race had over 50,000 runners. Some were noticeably bigger, faster and better prepared than I was. I noticed some seemed even better equipped with headphones, expensive running shoes, and fashionable athletic attire.

Similarly, close to one million businesses will be started in any given year. Some of these businesses are bigger and faster than others. Some of them are better prepared than their peers. Some of these start-ups are even better equipped than other new businesses with high-tech offices, well-trained staff, and plenty of cash reserves in the bank.

As the race started, I was initially disappointed because the pace was so slow. The first quarter of a mile we walked. Slowly, the pace picked up to a slow jog. Finally, after the first mile, we were able to hit our stride. Even then, the pace of the run was sporadic as we went up and down hills, around slower runners, and periodically stopped for water.

Starting a business is the same way. Very rarely do our actual sales in the first months or first year match our revenue forecasts. Often small business owners are far too optimistic about the pace of their start-up. They don't anticipate the peaks and valleys. They don't expect to have to maneuver around their competitors. They don't imagine that they will run low on cash and have to acquire additional financial resources to keep the business running.

It wasn't until the end of the fourth mile that I began to gain the confidence I needed to finish the race. No matter what, I knew I could survive the final two miles. I had momentum. I had settled into a comfortable stride that I felt I could maintain to the finish.

It wasn't until the end of the third year of my business that I felt that we had survived the worst. Research on small businesses has shown that the average small business doesn't show a profit until the third year. The majority of small businesses fail to make it to their fifth year.

As I approached the finish line I saw a number of other runners had stopped running. They were walking and even stumbling to the finish. They were determined to finish the race no matter what. They reminded me of so many small businesses I have witnessed. They, too, are tired, stumbling, and their resources are almost entirely drained. I often wonder what drives these people toward such pain and suffering? Why not stop? Why not ask for help?

At last I crossed the finish line. I was filled with mixed emotions. I was ecstatic about finishing my first Peachtree Road Race. I was proud that all of my training and preparation had paid off. I was overwhelmed and humbled by the standing ovation the runners received from the huge crowd assembled at the end of the race.

I was also worried that this was just the first of many races. I knew I needed to improve my training and my skills in order to improve my time. I was also fearful this could be the last race I finish as the aging process will begin to take its toll.

Three days later I was back on the streets training for the next race.

During the fifth year of my business, we finally achieved our sales projection. Once again, I remember having mixed emotions. I was euphoric over achieving our sales goal. We had an office party and celebrated. I was proud of the business we had built and the people who made it possible. There was no standing ovation, but the look of achievement in the eyes of our employees gave me that same goofy feeling.

I was also worried. I worried that this was just the first time we had achieved our annual sales goal and that we needed to continue to grow the business and improve our ways if we were to remain competitive in the market. I was also fearful that we did not have the financial and intellectual capital to continue to prosper.

The next day I opened up the office just as I had each working day for the previous five years. Just another race....

"Experience is a hard teacher because she gives us the test first, the lesson afterwards."

~ VERNON LAW, BASEBALL PLAYER

A STRATEGIC BUSINESS PLAN HELPS ENSURE SWEET SUCCESS

July 2002

Quick: Name a product or service that you or your business will gain more satisfaction from while it's being developed or produced than when it's finished.

Your answer?

"My tax return?"

Wrong answer....

"Chocolate chip cookies?"

You're getting much closer....

"I give up."

Your strategic business plan.

"I never would have said that."

Well, don't feel embarrassed. Most business owners and managers do not consider developing a **Strategic Business Plan** for their organization. In fact, less than 20% of all small businesses have any type of plan in place. These include operating plans, marketing plans, succession plans, etc.

They deny themselves such pleasure for a number of reasons:

- It's far too difficult to do.

- It's far too costly to do.

- I don't have the time.

Imagine that you have hired a builder to construct your dream home. You have this rather vague picture of a house in your mind and you communicate this image to the builder.

Now imagine that your builder plunges into the construction of your home without any architectural plans or drawings.

In a panic, you stop construction and ask the builder why he isn't using any plans or drawings.

He responds, "It's far too difficult to do," or "It's far too costly to have done," or "I don't have the time."

It would be *crazy* to build a home without plans. How long would that "dream house" of yours last if it was not built to any type of specifications? How long do you think *your* business will last without any direction or strategy?

Now back to my original question.

What is fascinating about developing a business plan is that the greatest satisfaction comes from the development of the plan itself. It is just like baking chocolate chip cookies. I get more enjoyment from eating the delicious cookie dough while I'm baking than I do from the baked goods upon completion. Sometimes I get halfway done baking and stop completely. On a rare occasion the dough never makes it to the oven.

The business plan development process includes the following three steps:

1. Analyze the business, as it exists at that moment in time.

2. Determine your 3–5 year vision for the business.

3. Decide what you need to do to move toward that vision

As you go through this process you will be forced to examine your business, as you have probably never done before. You will uncover your strengths and weaknesses. You will identify market opportunities and threats. You will set goals and objectives and then establish an action plan geared to achieving them.

You will take the image of your "dream house" out of your head and onto paper where it belongs.

When you finish, you will feel exhilarated and motivated like never before. You will find new confidence in your business. If this is not the case, it's time to bail out. Sell the farm.

Once your business plan is completed, it then becomes your road map for leading your business. You will use it to make sure that the "construction" of your business is just as you have planned for. You may even want to share it with others such as your employees, your banker, or even your family.

Just like chocolate chip cookies.

*"There is no failure in not realizing
all that you might dream;
the failure is not dreaming all
that you might realize."*

~ D. Hoc

Too Busy? Take a Vacation.

August 2002

Do you know what the most productive day of the year is for the typical business owner or manager?

Mondays? Maybe for some. Pay day? No. Labor Day? Just kidding….

It's the day **before** you take vacation. This little known fact has actually been researched and documented. *Why is this so?*

I just returned from my family's vacation week at the beach. I had my fill of fast food, sun tan lotion, and long walks on the beach. Several days before our departure, I honestly never thought I would finish the work that had stacked up on my desk—proposals to complete, projects to finish, phone calls to make. There were Post-it reminders all over my desk threatening to take my entire workspace hostage.

Then it happened. All week I had made considerable progress on my work but I was certain that I would end up stuffing my briefcase with leftover work and dragging it to the beach for its completion. When I woke up the day before our departure, I was like a man possessed. I started by taking an inventory of every task I needed to finish by the end of the day. Next, I wrote an action plan for the day listing each task and estimating the time needed for completion. I then prioritized the list based on each task's relative importance. I also grouped activities by the type of technology necessary for completion, i.e., telephone, computer, automobile. There was not a second to waste.

I even found myself tackling several tasks I had procrastinated on for weeks. It just seemed to make sense to tie up all the loose ends. I also made several new and follow-up client contacts. I had been putting them off for way too long.

Each call was very productive. Why had I been putting off these inquiries?

I actually finished all of my tasks by mid-afternoon. I had time to spare. Time to pack and begin lugging out all of the beach paraphernalia. The chairs and buckets seem to multiply like jackrabbits each year.

What is it about going away on vacation that creates such a mentality of urgency? For me, I believe it is due to several factors:

1. Not wanting to take work with me on vacation.

2. A concern that I may never return from vacation (I draw a mental picture of Jaws), and the desire to make sure all of my pending tasks are either completed or on schedule.

3. A strong desire to leave town on a very positive note: Projects completed. Customers contacted. Fires extinguished.

4. A strong desire not to return from vacation on a negative note: Projects behind schedule. Clients complaining. Numerous four-alarm fires.

Zig Ziglar, a famous motivational speaker and author, provided several reasons why individuals are so productive the day before vacation in his book, *Over The Top*. First, such individuals tend to set goals for that day which then require a high level of commitment. Next, he found that they tend to get started early in the day on achieving these goals. He also found that they tend to work with a higher level of enthusiasm on the day before vacation, which can't help but impact their productivity. We are also far less likely to procrastinate this day as well. Instead, we focus on finishing one task or project before leaping into the next one. What a novel thought....

In his research Ziglar also took note of the fact that people tend to do the "tough" jobs early on the day before vacation. He reasons that "If you have to swallow a frog, why waste time looking at it?"

On the day before vacation workers also tend to be extremely focused and disciplined in their efforts, according to Ziglar. Rather than looking for interruptions in their work, they avoid them as much as possible. There is too much stuff to get done and too little time to waste.

What impact will your individual efforts on this day have on your employees or co-workers? It's possible that they may wish you had left on vacation one day earlier. More than likely, it is your commitment, enthusiasm, and determination that will become contagious. It will have a multiplier effect across the organization as others feel the impact of your robust level of productivity.

That leaves us with one remaining question. Is it possible to apply this "day before vacation" mentality and use it, with caution, every day? Can we create the same level of urgency, enthusiasm, and commitment five days a week, fifty weeks a year? Why not? I need some time to consider these questions. I need some time to further mull over the application of my findings. I need... another vacation.

"Life is like a one-speed bicycle.
Most of us have gears we never use."

~ CHARLES SCHULZ

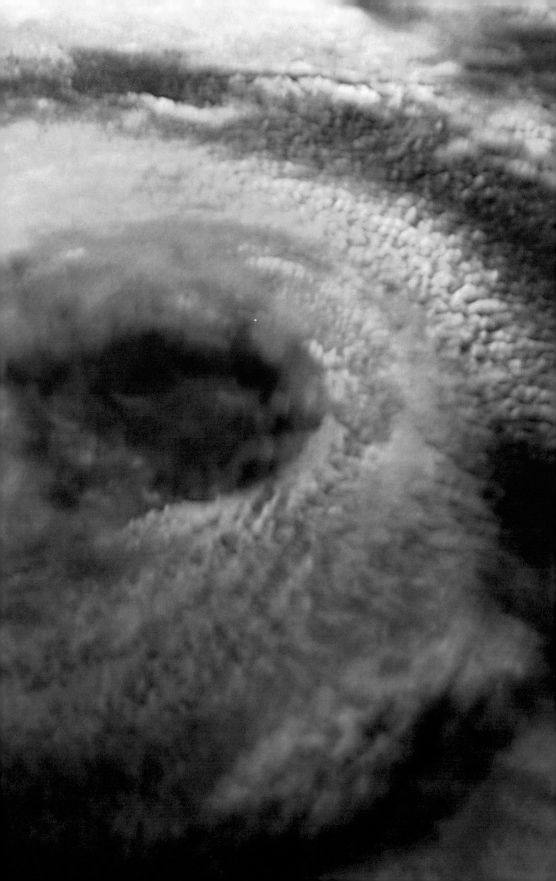

FIVE LESSONS LEARNED
FROM HURRICANE ANDREW

September 2002

Ten years ago, Hurricane Andrew assaulted south Florida. I lived and owned a business in the city of Homestead, Florida, which was hardest hit by the storm. Over the past ten years I have had considerable time to ponder the lessons I learned before, during, and after the hurricane. From the perspective of a small business owner, I have identified five lessons that will stay with me for a lifetime.

Hurricane Andrew was a Category 5 monster with winds exceeding 145 mph. It was the most costly weather disaster in U.S. history. It inflicted over $25 billion in damages in south Florida. It killed 15 people in Miami-Dade County and was indirectly responsible for at least 25 other deaths. The storm destroyed over 25,000 homes (mine included) and damaged over 100,000 additional houses. At least 180,000 people were temporarily left homeless.

After the hurricane we had 23,000 soldiers and 6000 members of the National Guard move into our neighborhood. Helicopters flew in formation. Convoys thundered through residential streets and over massive amounts of debris. There were military checkpoints where busy traffic intersections used to be. Schools were destroyed. Common landmarks such as trees, buildings, and signs were gone. I got lost in my own subdivision. It was a scene I can't even begin to compare anything to.

Within days of the storm, we decided to rebuild our home and our business in their original locations. We knew both efforts were going to be huge challenges. We had no idea just how challenging they would be.

For six months we operated our travel agency out of a trailer in a gravel parking lot behind where the building once stood. The hurricane relocated most of our files, airline tickets, and small office equipment somewhere west of us in the Everglades National Park. We worked with temporary phones, makeshift desks, and a port-a-let. Getting to work each day was a minor miracle. Making it through each day required extraordinary patience and resilience.

By the time we were able to move into our new office and resume some level of normalcy, a number of rather simple business lessons were learned.

Lesson #1: Carefully pick your business partners. When I speak to individuals starting new businesses I talk about the importance of selecting the right external professionals for their respective business start-ups. We discuss the importance of finding professionals such as an attorney, an accountant, and a banker who understand your business. It is imperative that you, the business owner, are able to establish some level of chemistry with these professionals.

After the hurricane we were very fortunate, particularly in terms of our bank and our insurance company. Both partners worked very hard to help us through the painful recovery stage of the storm and then the rebuilding efforts. Their interest in us was not only because we were business clients, but we were people and neighbors as well.

Our landlord was a different story. Our landlord decided to capitalize on this disaster as a business opportunity. While other business vendors and suppliers went to great lengths to work with us as partners in rebuilding, this individual was difficult to work with and took advantage of his own insurance company and us at the same time. Lesson learned….

Lesson #2: The importance of customer loyalty. Prior to the hurricane I had attended numerous customer service seminars and had been told how important customer satisfaction was to our business. It made sense, but the theory had never really been tested until after the storm.

We found out that many of our clients were not just satisfied customers; they were extremely loyal to our business. How did we know this? Due to the circumstances at this time, our customers had to go to great lengths to use our service. We did not have dependable phone service, or power for a while.

Instead our customers had to come find our office trailer. There was no parking per se, or even a waiting area. There were no comfortable chairs, and air conditioning was minimal. It was literally an ordeal to come to our office for any of our customers.

And yet they came. Day after day we saw more and more old customers show up. Some just came by to see if we were okay. Some were planning their exodus from south Florida. Others had insurance checks and were planning getaway vacations. Our business clients slowly began to travel again.

I am convinced that we did **not** see too many of our previously *satisfied* customers. I have come to understand that satisfied customer will switch brands very easily if the price is right or the switching costs are minimal. No, the loyal customers came back to us after the storm. They felt an emotional connection to our agency and our employees that made switching agencies almost impossible. That is a lesson I won't forget….

Lesson #3: The importance of employee loyalty. This lesson is similar to the previous one. I had studied employee motivation and leadership for many years before Hurricane Andrew. I prided myself on being an effective leader. Many of our employees had been with us for a considerable amount of time. They seemed to be satisfied with their employment. They seemed to be loyal to their employers, but that loyalty had never really been tested until then.

After the hurricane, our immediate concerns were with the safety and well-being of our employees. Many of them experienced the same level of damage to their homes as we had. A number of them had to relocate to hotels, rental homes, or other family residences for months. Some had better insurance than others. Some faced significant financial hardship as a result of the storm. Like us, each of them was trying to figure out how such a bad thing could happen to such good people.

The miracle was that within almost a week of the disaster, each of our employees was prepared to return to work. Not because they had to, but because they wanted to. At this point in time, our office was as close to a home as they had and we were all family. This was not easy work. For a time every booking was done manually without computers. There was a very high level of stress due to the situation and the clients we were serving. Had it not been for these loyal employees we would have never been able to rebuild the business as we did. Many of the items we lost during and after the hurricane were replaceable. These individuals were not replaceable. They were one of a kind.

Loyalty is like beauty; it's very hard to describe, but you know it when you see it.

Lesson #4: Don't ever under-insure your business or home. The aftermath of Hurricane Andrew was a classic learning experience in the field of insurance. For years I had taken our business insurance coverage for granted. Every year our agent would pay us a visit and would present us with our insurance coverage (bill). I can't say that I truly understood what was covered and what wasn't. Over the years I had processed a handful of claims and never had reason to question what we had or didn't have in our coverage.

The year prior to the hurricane we met with our agent as usual. We were looking for ways to cut costs, and asked that he take a little known coverage called Business Interruption Insurance off of our bill. We thought that $150 savings could be applied somewhere else in the business. Our agent politely replied that if we did not want that coverage then we would have to find another insurance agent. He stated that he could not sell us that policy in good conscience without that coverage. Rather than switch insurance agents, we buckled and took the policy as presented. Thank goodness.

We later came to find out that Business Interruption Insurance protects the owner's earnings from the business in case the operation of the business is interrupted due to a storm, a disaster, war, etc. This coverage provided my family with income for one year as we built our business back to where it was the business day before the storm. In addition, we were fortunate that we had provided ourselves with excellent contents insurance. This allowed us to replace all of the equipment, furnishings, etc. in our office. Needless to say, I am now a proponent of Business Interruption Insurance.

Lesson #5: At the end of the game all the pieces go back in the box. This is the one lesson that has had the greatest impact on me since Hurricane Andrew. Leading up to the day of impact, I had worked very hard for ten years to build a portfolio of personal and business assets. In less than twenty-four hours, the majority of those tangible assets had been lost. Sure, we were able to recover certain items that had not been destroyed by the storm or ruined by the days of rain that followed. Yes, insurance allowed us to rebuild and start over. However, this thought stayed with me—the tokens we work so hard to earn could be lost abruptly, and, in our case, due to no fault of our own. Even if we make it to a ripe old age, much of what we have collected gets redistributed anyway.

What the storm couldn't take away are those things that I value *most* today: family, friends, and a lifetime of great memories.

"Life isn't about waiting for the storm to pass. It's about learning to dance in the rain."

~ VIVIAN GREENE

Business plan

...in the state of Texas. This corporation is a p... ...older and one ...cipal investor, Regina Wager... ...er ...d the sponsoring broker for this firm. The lic... ...m... licensed real estate agents... ...z ...rporation will formalize... ...dent c...

TEN REASONS WHY MOST BUSINESS PLANS FAIL... AND WHAT TO DO ABOUT IT

November 2002

Last month we examined the strategic planning process. Research indicates that less than 20% of small businesses execute any type of business plan. Research also indicates that only about 20% of all small businesses survive their first five years. Is that a coincidence? I don't think so.

Unfortunately, for the few brave and courageous business owners who do develop a plan for their business, many of their business plans fail. While their intent is good, the results are disappointing. Why? Here are ten reasons:

Reason #1: The plan does not start with an end in mind.
Your plan's development should start with a determination of the organization's primary aim. Why are you in business? The remainder of the business plan should flow from that statement of purpose. As Steven Covey states in his best-selling book, *Seven Habits of Highly Effective People*, "Begin with the end in mind." If you take a trip, your first and possibly most important decisions are: Where am I going? What is my destination? That is your primary aim. You then establish objectives, goals, and strategies that will keep you driving toward your pre-selected destination.

Reason #2: The plan is incomplete.
Your business plan must include certain information that may be required by individuals outside of the organization. This would include bankers, investors, channel partners, etc. These items may include prior years' financials, resumes for top management, a history of the business, and an analysis of the competition. While this information may not be relevant to your development of the business, it might be very important to people outside of your business that make critical decisions about your company based on this plan.

31

Reason #3: The plan is too long and difficult to read.
Your plan typically should not exceed 15–20 pages. Nothing turns off a banker more than to have your version of *War and Peace* sitting right in front of him. Be concise. The plan should be written in layman's terms. The appearance of the plan is important. This document should be the most powerful selling tool you have. It should persuade the reader to think that your company is successful today and will continue to be so in the future. The appearance of the document should reflect that intent. If necessary, have it typeset.

Reason #4: Only the business owner or top management develops the plan.
This is the *business* plan, not the *owner's* plan. If you expect the participation of the employees in the execution of the plan, you must involve them in the development of the document. Your employees should also be involved in the timely evaluation of the business plan. Their input will be invaluable to you as you evaluate and update your plan.

Reason #5: The plan lacks adequate "front-end" analysis.
Your business plan should be based on a thorough analysis of your business using a S.W.O.T. approach: **S**trengths, **W**eaknesses, **O**pportunities, and **T**hreats. The identification of these factors will enable you to determine the appropriate goals and strategies your plan must include in order for you to reach your primary aim. Before we go on our "trip" we always check to see that the "roads" are safe and the vehicle is "well-tuned."

Reason #6: The plan is written for the sole purpose of raising capital.
Such a one-dimensional plan is sure to fail. Your plan should serve as map by which you can reach your organization's primary aim. You will then want to share this document with anyone who has a significant stake in your business. These stakeholders may include your employees, your creditors, your banker, and even your customers. Each of these stakeholder groups has a vital interest in the direction of your company and should be taken into consideration when developing your business plan.

Reason #7: The plan is written, approved, and filed for safekeeping until next year.
Your plan should be reviewed, evaluated, and updated regularly. The development of the plan should be an ongoing process. I suggest that you write the plan annually, review it monthly, and update it quarterly. Do not hesitate to change

your plan if necessary. If you decide to change your direction or destination, make sure you also change your map.

Reason #8: The plan's financial projections are unrealistic.
Your plan should include financial projections that are accurate, reasonable, and attainable. These numbers should be based on hard data. Loan officers are trained to reduce revenue projections by 50% and double certain expense projections. This is particularly true for a new business due to a lack of past financial performance. For an existing business, your financial projections should be based on historical data, your situational analysis, and growth expectations. Be prepared to defend your financial forecast and its underlying assumptions.

Reason #9: The plan is not balanced in its attention to the primary functions of the business.
Your business plan should address all three of the primary functions of the organization: marketing, operations, and finance. Each area may not be of equal importance to your company, however, all three functions are interrelated. A lack of attention or planning in one area might significantly impact one or both of the other areas. Remember, your organizational chain is only as strong as the weakest link. The development of strong links starts with the business plan.

Reason #10: The plan is dependent upon people for the business to be successful.
Your plan should create a system of doing business. The system then provides jobs for people. Remember, the true value of a business is based not on what it sells, but how it sells it. McDonald's has been successful, not because of its hamburgers, but because of the McDonald's system which provides a consistent and predictable level of service to its customers.

"The nicest thing about not planning is that failure comes as a complete surprise and is not preceded by a period of worry and depression."

~RICHARD PALMER

CUSTOMERS FOR LIFE?

January 2003

My thirteen-year old son Taylor received an interesting lesson in customer service this week. About six months ago he opened his first bank account. He has been earning money doing odd jobs and collecting a weekly allowance. As I saw mounds of cash accruing on his bedroom desk, I suggested he open a bank account to secure these hard-earned monies.

I took Taylor down to the bank and he opened his own checking account. In my youth, banks had special accounts for kids with minimal service charges. This mega-bank had no such account so he opened a basic checking account. Taylor couldn't wait until he got his own debit card. He envisioned endless streams of cash being disbursed by ATMs conveniently located around the city.

After the first of the year, school and baseball began to demand more of his time. He began to drain what little savings he had built months earlier. The account remained dormant for several months. Taylor began to collect the monthly bank statements and he carefully analyzed each one. He wanted to make sure they hadn't carelessly misplaced someone else's deposits in his account like he had seen in the movies and on television.

As the summer break began, Taylor once again began to accumulate some money as a result of his entrepreneurial efforts. As the funds began to stack up on his desk, I again suggested he make a deposit. He filled out the deposit slip and then trusted dad to put his $84 in the bank.

I pulled into the drive-thru at the bank, inserted Taylor's deposit into the aerodynamic container, and away it went. Several minutes passed and a friendly voice welcomed me to the bank. After sharing her well-scripted welcome, she then informed me that this account was closed.

"Is there anything else I can do for you today Mr. Fulton?" she inquired in a voice borrowed from a bad Disney cartoon.

"Account closed? How can that be?" I responded.

She was not able to answer my question. She did, however, invite me to park my car and waltz right into the bank lobby as if I hadn't already been tortured enough by this experience. I thought not. I decided that I would rather vent from the confines of my home office. There I could yell and scream without total strangers looking at me like I was some type of wild man on a mission from hell.

On my way home I began to consider how this could happen. What would lead this billion-dollar banking gorilla to close my young son's only hope for financial independence? Why was there no notification? No letter or phone call?

My only guess was that due to the inactivity the bank must do a clean sweep of certain accounts each month. What savings does this achieve? Is there an expense to keeping such accounts open?

In customer service training I talk about the lifetime value of a client. I now considered what the lifetime value of this thirteen-year-old client was. My conservative guess is that he might deposit approximately $3–5 million over the next 70 years. He is likely to borrow about that same amount over the same period of time. What is the potential earning the bank would receive as a result of this activity? My guess is about the same amount of $3–5 million. This figure represents the lifetime value of this young customer to this financial institution.

As a result of closing this young man's first bank account, this bank had chosen to hand that potentially lucrative business over to one of its competitors. How considerate. That amount doesn't even include the multiplier effect when this incident gets communicated via word-of-mouth.

What is the lifetime value of your customers?

Training Magazine reported in October about a casino in Wisconsin that estimates its guests are worth almost $350,000 each, without the multiplier effect. Carl Sewell, author and famous Cadillac car dealership owner, estimated once that each of his customers had a lifetime value of over $300,000. This estimate was based on each customer buying twelve cars at $25,000 a piece over a lifetime. Michael Hurst owns a seafood restaurant in Fort Lauderdale, Florida. He figured that if one guest spends $50 a year at his restaurant and sends two friends, who then send two friends each, and so on, the ten-year value of the first customer is $1,476,200.

I am wondering if that casino turns away customers who haven't visited in a while. Does the car dealership refuse to sell a new car to a customer who has delayed his purchase for a period of time? Can you imagine the restaurant refusing service to the patron who had stayed home for a while?

What are you doing to find, capture, and retain lifetime customers? Are you closing their account(s) due to a slip in activity? I hope not. That's not only stupid. It's entrepreneurial suicide.

"Profit is the applause you get from appreciative customers and committed employees."

~ KEN BLANCHARD, AUTHOR

Uncertain Times in Customer Service

February 2003

Two weeks ago, my wife and I ventured off to see a movie. Such opportunities are rare for us and we were looking forward to the time away from the house to see this highly-rated movie. About halfway through the movie, a fire alarm was set off, the house lights came on, and the movie came to a screeching halt.

Next came an interesting display of human behavior. About a third of the audience went racing out of the theater in fear of being scorched. Another third, including us, stood up and moved out to the aisles, not really sure what to do. The remaining portion of the audience stayed in their seats, munching hour-old popcorn and wondering what the fuss was about.

Those of us that stayed waited for directions from the theater management. Should we exit? Should we stay? How long would the delay be? Thirty minutes passed and there was not a single communication from anyone associated with the theater. Several patrons ventured out into the lobby and found out there had not been a fire. Theater personnel were attempting to revive the screenings.

The most aggravating thing about this entire situation was not the wait. We just assumed that there would be a delay prior to the continuation of the film. What was most upsetting about this situation was the *uncertainty* we faced as customers of this establishment. How long would the delay be? Would refunds be made available if we chose to leave? What caused the interruption?

I was reminded of one of my favorite quotes in the field of customer service:

"Customers don't measure service in terms of minutes, instead customer service is measured in degrees of uncertainty."

What could the theater have done differently? A theater representative should have addressed the audience within several minutes of the disruption, explained the nature of the delay and the approximate wait time. I am confident that the vast majority of the customers would have been quite satisfied with that effort and would have stayed for the remainder of the show. Instead, a significant number of patrons left the theater and those of us that stayed were not "happy campers."

I have been a victim of these instances of customer *dis-service* on many occasions. So have you. It happens at airports, restaurants, auto repair shops, and many other places. The uncertainty may be related to product delivery, follow-up, payment due, employee changes, and in some cases, the viability of the provider. Rather than step up and be pro-active in their communication with customers, companies instead decide that their customers are better off not knowing what's going on. They don't trust customers to make good decisions based on good information. What a shame.

Employers are also guilty of doing this to their internal customers. Employees are often uncertain as to why and how key decisions are being made. They are kept waiting to know how and when to proceed with a given task. Again, employees don't measure their manager's effectiveness by the length of the delay, but instead by the amount of uncertainty at hand.

What can you do to minimize the amount of uncertainty your customers face?

- **Act quickly.** When there is a service issue with a customer, such as an interruption in service, the key is to communicate with the customer as quickly and as honestly as possible. Help the customer understand the nature of the problem, what you are doing to address the problem, and how long they can expect to wait for a remedy.

- **Over-communicate** with your internal and external customers using a variety of media. Effective communication helps build trust and confidence with your customers in preparation for the day that there is that inevitable service issue.

- **Implement internal controls** that ensure that customers are not left "in the dark" when facing a problem with your product/service offering. In my example at the movie theater, there should have been procedures to follow when a fire alarm goes off. There should have been instructions for theater personnel as to how and when to communicate with patrons if there is a fire alarm.

• **Training.** Make sure your employees understand the destructive impact "uncertainty" has on levels of customer satisfaction and loyalty. In addition, train your employees how to alleviate your client's feelings of uncertainty.

I believe that customer *uncertainty* translates into diminishing client loyalty. I will return to that movie theater if it is the only option to see a movie of choice. Otherwise, I will shift my movie ticket dollars to another venue where I am more *certain* of the quality of customer care.

"If you listen closely enough, your customers will explain your business to you."

~ PETER SCHUTZ

Do You Have the Magic?

April 2003

The requirements of a successful company CEO are numerous and have been well-documented by many authors far more notable than me. However, my experience working with thousands of small business owners over the past twenty years has shown me that the most successful CEOs must have no one outstanding attribute. Instead they must possess a blend of competencies designated by the acronym **MAGIC**. They include:

- **M**aking good decisions
- Being **A**ccountable
- Possessing a continual thirst for personal and professional **G**rowth
- Ability to manage **I**solation
- Capable of managing **C**hange

Let's examine each of these critically important CEO competencies.

As a business leader you will be confronted with making key strategic decisions on a regular basis. How do you **make decisions**? Is there a process in place for handling the tough issues that you are faced with? Are you in a group that provides you with guidance and support when making these difficult choices?

I find that many CEOs are incapable of making these decisions for a variety of reasons. These include lack of experience, lack of confidence, and an inability to follow their "gut." Often we know what the right course of action is, but we are hesitant to take the necessary "leap of faith" that is required to be an effective leader.

As a result the CEO is stymied by these decisions. He or she is held hostage by their own inability to take action. Their CEO currency is diminished as their followers witness them floundering in their own wading pool of indecisiveness.

The CEO must also hold themselves **accountable** for the performance of their company. We have seen too many examples recently of CEOs not exercising this responsibility and becoming engulfed in scandals that crushed their companies. Examples of these include Enron, Anderson, and WorldCom to name just a few.

Many CEOs I speak to relish the thought of becoming more accountable. I also felt this way as the owner/operator of several small businesses. I wanted to be held to a greater level of accountability. I was good at holding my employees accountable to key performance metrics. We had quarterly performance reviews and it was clear what they were accountable for, and what the consequences were, if they did not perform up to those expectations.

But what about me? Who was I accountable to? My employees? My customers? My family? The answer to each of these questions is yes, but the problem was that none of these key stakeholders chose to hold me accountable. This is true for many CEOs as well. At the end of the day you must, first and foremost, hold yourself accountable. You must take responsibility for your own actions, your own job performance, and your own decision-making.

The good news is that there is help in this area. Many CEOs have enlisted the support of executive coaches, advisory groups, or peer CEO groups like TEC (The Executive Committee) to help hold them accountable.

CEOs must also provide themselves with opportunities for professional and personal **growth**. You may be prepared to start a business, but do you have the professional skills required to run a successful $5–10M company? You may have all the skills necessary to run this small business, but are you prepared to take it to the next growth stage? Many CEOs are not.

How much time and money do you budget for professional and personal growth in a year? The most successful business leaders have a thirst for knowledge. They are continually reading books, listening to tapes, and attending classes. They understand that they cannot stunt their own intellectual growth and expect their business to grow. Companies that embrace professional growth will invest 5–10% of annual revenues into training and development, and then typically see a 5:1 return on that investment.

We are even guiltier of ignoring our personal growth. When was the last time you took a class or read a book on maintaining your health/fitness, or building relationships, or just something fun? I am confident there is not just a balance between work and our personal lives, but rather a blend between the two. The same is true of our development in these two areas of our lives. They are inseparable and must be nourished on a regular basis.

When surveyed, many CEOs report a deep and sometimes-painful feeling of isolation as the head of their businesses and typically their families as well. Why is this? As a business owner, I always felt it was important to separate myself from my employees. I did not socialize with my employees as a general rule. The less I knew of their personal lives and they of mine, the better off we all were, I assumed. This philosophy created a natural and comfortable division between my employees and I.

Is this isolation healthy? For most it is not. It can cause an unhealthy level of stress. More importantly for now is the question of how the CEO manages that isolation. For some it is by building strong personal and professional relationships outside of the business. This may be a Saturday golf group, involvement in church, or joining a CEO peer group. The key is to identify and execute strategies that will begin to alleviate these feelings of isolation.

The final component of **MAGIC** is the ability to adapt to **change**. How do you prepare for and manage the changes that take place within your business, your industry, and your life? For most, we live in the reactive mode. We react to changes in our business and our personal lives with a knee-jerk and wonder why we had not been better prepared.

Successful CEOs understand the need to prepare for change and remain proactive in their preparation. They seek out industry speakers. They attend conferences and trade shows. They continually push themselves to stay on the cutting edge of industry trends, emerging technology, and new market opportunities. Rather than being averse to change, they seek opportunities for change. This compelling change mentality also then becomes contagious within their respective organizations.

MAGIC… Five key competencies that differentiate the great CEOs from the rest of the pack. Despite the acronym, there is no magic in their success. No smoke or mirrors. Instead they have the courage to lead, the stamina to endure the peaks and valleys of entrepreneurship, and the willingness to ask for and provide support. Dedicate yourself to working in each of these five areas and the results will be… **MAGICAL,** of course.

"Take 10 minutes right now and ask yourself, 'What one thing should I do tomorrow that will have the biggest impact on my business?' And then don't stop until it's done."

~ KEITH MCFARLAND

Customer Loyalty vs. Satisfaction: Is There a Difference?

August 2003

I spent time recently with one of my clients who had just recently spent considerable time and resources to survey the satisfaction levels of his respective customers and employees. The results were in and overall they were very positive for both internal (employee) and external customer groups.

But the client had mixed emotions. While he was pleased with the ratings indicating high levels of customer satisfaction, he was disappointed that his customer and employee turnover rates continued to be very high despite these recent findings.

"How could that be?" he asked. "Is it possible that satisfied customers would leave me?"

The answer to his question is a resounding **YES!**

Why? Satisfied customers will stay until there is a better alternative offered to them. This is true for both external and internal customer groups. When ex-customers are surveyed in exit interviews, they typically reveal that they left because they received a better deal or offer. They did not feel committed to the prior company because there was no emotional connection.

On the other hand, loyal customers are a different breed. Loyal customers will stay with you as long as possible. **The mistake we make is confusing loyal customers with satisfied customers.** A lot of research over the years has indicated that there is no connection between customer loyalty and customer satisfaction. None. Just because a customer indicates a high level of satisfaction does not mean that they are, or will be, loyal to you. Customer loyalty entails an emotional state of mind. You have imbedded yourself in the heart and mind of that customer.

Here are two examples. I am satisfied with my gas station. It is the closest station to my house and is located on a convenient corner for me to stop by when my gas tank is almost empty. The store is clean. The people are friendly. I have yet to experience bad service there. Yet, I would never go out of my way to fill up there. At least half of the time I end up purchasing gas somewhere else during the week. I have no guilt whatsoever for doing so. If this station closed I would painlessly go to the station across the street.

When it comes to a great steak dinner, I am very loyal to Hal's. Why? First, they have great food with outstanding service accompanied by a terrific dining ambience. But more importantly I feel an emotional tie to this restaurant. When I first considered moving to Atlanta I came to visit the city and spent my first evening with friends at Hal's. We had a remarkable dining experience. Ever since then, I find myself returning for special occasions such as birthdays, anniversaries, and entertaining friends who are in town. I am certain that the employees at Hal's don't know me, but I know them. When I am there I feel at home. I recommend this eating establishment whenever possible. If they were to close, I would feel genuinely saddened. In Ken Blanchard's terms, I am a "Raving Fan" of this dining establishment.

What is the difference between the gas station and the restaurant? It's all on the *emotional* level. In order to get my loyalty you need to engage my mind and pierce my heart. It's that simple.

How can you differentiate between your satisfied customers and your loyal customers? Here are eight ways. They are equally relevant to your external customers as they are to your internal employee customers. ?

#1: Pricing. You negotiate prices with satisfied customers. You negotiate costs with loyal customers.

#2: Payment. Satisfied customers pay at their discretion. Loyal customers pay on time.

#3: Referrals. Satisfied customers become referrals to your competitors. Loyal customers willingly provide referrals to you.

#4: Turnover. Generally, you will experience turnover rates of 15% or higher with satisfied customers. The turnover rate for loyal customers will be less than 15% and it will be for reasons outside of your control.

#5: Competitive data. Your satisfied customers seek competitive data. Your loyal customers are sharing competitive data.

#6: Perception. Satisfied customers perceive you as a commodity provider. Loyal customers perceive you as a partner.

#7: Contract. You will need a contract to keep many satisfied customers in place. You have a virtual lifetime contract with your loyal customers.

#8: Difficult times. Satisfied customers will leave you. Loyal customers will stay by your side.

My advice to my client is maybe it's time to *stop* measuring customer satisfaction and *start* tracking customer loyalty. **There is a difference.**

"A relationship is not something that you pursue; it's what happens to you when you are immersed in serving the dreams of your customer."

~ TOM PETERS

Blocking and Tackling
in the Game of Business

September 2003

My dad used to love the old Green Bay Packers. Coach Vince Lombardi was an icon in his mind. The reason he was so enamored with the Packers was the way they won football games. They won the old-fashioned way he used to say. That meant they won games because they did two things better than their opponents: *blocking and tackling.* They had players like Jerry Kramer on the offensive line and Ray Nitchzke on defense who were the best in their respective positions at football basics. As a result they didn't have to rely solely on a skilled quarterback, a wide receiver, or a kicker to always make the big plays in order to win games. The games were won "in the trenches," as the broadcasters would always say to remind us.

I remember reading once about Lombardi and those great Packer teams. The article described how consumed Lombardi was with practicing the football basics. His teams spent almost all of their practice time working on and perfecting their blocking and tackling skills. They would do an endless number of drills from sunrise to late at night, just focusing on these key skills. Lombardi knew if his teams didn't excel in these key areas they would never be able to continue to enjoy the level of success they had attained. He knew he didn't necessarily have any more talented players than the rest of the teams in the league.

My youngest son is playing little league football for the first time this fall. His team practiced the first three weeks without ever touching a football. All they did was work on the fundamentals of blocking and tackling. Their coach understood, as Lombardi did, that if they can't execute these basic skills at a very high level, they would never excel at scoring points and winning football games.

I recently heard a retired CEO, from an internationally known company, talk about the importance of *blocking and tackling* in business. He explained that the key to his success in leading this company was the ability of his employees to execute the fundamentals. In other words he said, "It was all about blocking and tackling." He had no superstars on the assembly line. Instead he spoke of "achieving extraordinary results from ordinary people," just as Coach Lombardi had done.

Recalling the famed Packers and hearing this CEO speaker led me to consider just what are the fundamentals of business? What is it that businesses should be practicing and drilling on just as Lombardi's teams did? Are there tasks such as *blocking and tackling* which are so repetitive and almost boring to watch, that many business leaders choose to ignore them, yet they are so critical to the success of the business?

For six years my wife and I owned and operated a retail travel agency. It was a successful business in a very tough industry that grew five-fold in five years. It was as profitable as one could be in the travel business. I was in charge of sales and marketing. In other words, I was in charge of making "big plays." I brought in the new accounts and went after the big groups for their travel. I hired independent sales representatives. With each "big play," there would be celebrations in our office. Needless to say, I enjoyed this position.

However, I can take little credit for the success of this business.

My wife oversaw the daily operations of the agency. She coached our agents on making sure that the phones were answered in a timely manner and in a proper way. She made sure that our customers' travel reservations were accurate and priced correctly. My wife made sure that our equipment and technology were performing at peak levels. Her work was not exciting, nor did it catch the attention of those around her, but it was absolutely fundamental to our success. I have come to realize that her work was to oversee the *blocking and tackling* within the office. My success in making "big plays" was directly related to her and her agents' ability to perform the fundamentals of the business. She could easily have worn a football cap and a whistle around her neck. We had our own Jerry Kramers and Ray Nitchzkes working for us at that time and we didn't even know it.

What about your business? Here are several questions to consider about the *blocking and tackling* within your organization:

- What are the basic, fundamental and repetitive activities performed within your business each day that make or break your team's ability to win or lose?

- How often do your players practice or train on these activities? Do you allow a "new player" to perform these activities without a minimal level of coaching and practice?

- How are you measuring the performance of your front-line players in these activities? Are there certain metrics you monitor just as football coaches count missed tackles and the number of quarterback sacks?

- How are these players being rewarded and recognized for this unglamorous work?

- Do you have a playbook (policies and procedures) in place that accurately describes how, when, and for whom these chores are to be performed?

My dad's favorite game of all time was the championship game in the late '60s between the Packers and the Cowboys played in the frozen tundra at Green Bay. This was a very close game from the outset between two rival teams. The outcome of the game came down to the end of the fourth quarter. The Packers had the ball on the Cowboys one-foot line with very little time left and fourth down. Their quarterback, Bart Starr, took the snap. Then he scored on a quarterback sneak, with no time left, and won the game. Starr was mobbed by his teammates.

This game was not won with a long pass or the fancy footwork of a runner. The game was won because one of the linemen created just enough space, with a great block, so that Starr could push himself over the goal line. Thousands of hours of practice and training had paid off handsomely at the end of that game. While I can't remember who the blocker was I am sure that quarterback Starr and Coach Lombardi most certainly did. That game was all about *blocking and tackling*. That's just the way my dad liked his football.

"Fatigue makes cowards of us all."

~ VINCE LOMBARDI

DON'T GAMBLE ON EMPLOYEE SELECTION

October 2003

Employee selection. No two words frighten small business owners more than these.

Why is this? Maybe it's because the selection process can be so time consuming. Maybe it's because the process can be so costly. Maybe it's because we are never quite sure we know how to select the *right* person for the position.

I believe the main reason so many small business owners and managers dread the thought of hiring new personnel is because they have made bad decisions in the past. The very thought of duplicating such decisions brings terror to their hearts.

Why is it that despite our good intentions, we still make bad decisions in selecting new employees?

The reason is simple. We usually base our decisions on the wrong set of information. This fact became very evident to me recently in talking to a small business owner. Bill had just about sworn off hiring any more new employees as a result of the horrible experiences he had recently gone through when trying to fill several vacant positions.

Bill had owned a small retail business for five years and had always struggled in hiring new employees. I asked Bill on what basis he made a hiring decision. His response included such common factors as appearance, communication skills, and past experience. He then shared with me his most important factor in hiring a new employee. It was his ability to predict their future behavior and performance in the position he was hiring them for.

I was glad to hear that Bill used such a criteria for hiring. Experts tell us predicting future performance is quite normal and a good practice in the selection process.

I then asked Bill how he was able to predict such future performance. He responded that he would often ask hypothetical questions such as, "If you were getting ready to close the store and a customer entered and demanded that you stay open for the next thirty minutes while she browsed for a future purchase, what would you do?"

Bill also suggested that he tried to determine an applicant's work attitudes and moral values during the interview. That information, he felt, was important in trying to predict future work habits.

Bill felt that despite getting great information asking such questions, for some reason many of his new hires did not perform the way he had imagined during the interview. In fact, several of his newly hired employees turned out to be just the opposite of what he had predicted during the selection process.

In talking to Bill, I also found out that he was a huge sports fan. He loved college football and confided to me that he was known to place a wager on one or two games a week. In fact, he bragged to me that he had earned enough money last year from betting on football games to pay for a recent week-long vacation to Florida for his family.

I asked Bill what he contributed his betting success to.

He responded that he had become very good at predicting the outcomes of football games, almost to the exact point spread. He was able to do this by studying each team's past performance in close detail. He would watch replays of their previous games. He would scrutinize their statistics. He would research how the teams had played under similar circumstances over the years.

In simple terms, Bill had created a science of predicting football game outcomes by looking at past team performances.

I asked Bill if it was possible to draw a parallel between predicting winning football teams and predicting the future behavior of a potential employee.

At first Bill had a confused look on his face. He was having a difficult time correlating the process of picking football game winners with the selection of productive employees. Slowly, a grin emerged on his face as he realized the connection between the two processes.

"Are you saying that I should pick my employees the same way that I pick my football games?" he asked.

"Absolutely," I responded.

All of a sudden Bill experienced a huge awakening. He realized that he would never bet on a football team just because the coach talked of winning such a game. He would never pick a team to win just because of their apparent work attitude or values. In picking his teams, he predicted future performance based on past behavior under similar circumstances. It had always worked. Why wouldn't it work in selecting new employees?

Of course it would.

Not only will it work for Bill, but it will also work for any business, large or small. Research has conclusively shown that the only way that we can accurately predict an employee's *future* behavior is by looking at their *past* behavior under *similar* circumstances.

Why is this so? Because *behavior* can be measured, it can be evaluated, and it can be changed. To the contrary, *attitude* is difficult to measure, evaluate, or change. Which one would you want to use to predict future performance?

If an employee has a history of satisfying customers in similar situations as your workplace would require, you can bet that same employee would continue at that same level of performance under your supervision. Likewise, if an applicant has had negative experiences in the past, you can rest assured that he or she will repeat that behavior in a future position.

So the formula is simple. We select employees on the basis of predicting their future performance as a result of their past behavior under similar circumstances. This formula has been tested many times in many different situations. It has always provided the *best* means to acquiring great employees.

I received a call from Bill last week. He had hired his first new employee using this new philosophy and he was certain that this young lady was going to be a star employee. In fact, in just a week's time she was setting a new standard in outstanding customer service for other employees to follow.

Bill was ecstatic. He couldn't wait to hire his next employee. He is also enjoying football this fall. He is certain that this would be a profitable season.

"You are only as competent as the weakest
key executive that reports to you."

~ MAURICE MASCARENHAS

ENTREPRENEURIAL HOLIDAY WISH LIST

December 2003

I just received Christmas wish lists from both of my sons and my wife. They all have very lofty expectations for this holiday season. I will do more than my part to stimulate the nation's economy by the time I am done shopping. I will be deep into government-like deficit spending by year-end.

I know that many of you have yet to complete your own holiday wish list, and I would like to provide several suggestions. Here we go:

1. **A portrait of your best customer.** This would hang right behind your desk to remind you and your followers why you are in business. Having a hard time making a tough business decision? Just turn around and consult the picture. What's in their best interest? Trying to make a difficult hiring decision? Would you want this applicant spending considerable time with this customer?

2. **A Greyhound bus miniature.** My wife gave me a little red sports car miniature several years ago because she said she could not afford to give me the real thing. Why a bus? Just a reminder of author Jim Collins', *Good To Great*, suggestion of your role as the bus driver in your company. As the bus driver you must make very important personnel decisions. It is your job to decide who gets on your bus and where they are to sit. You must also decide who doesn't get on the bus.

3. **The book *Good To Great* by Jim Collins.** I believe that this was the best read of the year. Keep it close to your desk for frequent reference. Consider how you measure up as a Level 5 Leader.

4. **A mirror.** Every once in a while we need to remind ourselves who is in charge. We forget and allow the patients to run the asylum. When things are going well look into that mirror and take credit. Likewise, when business takes a turn for the worse, pose for a brief time in front of that mirror and take responsibility for strategic action.

5. **A subscription to *Inc* magazine.** I consider *Inc* to be consistently the best reading for small business owners. Dare you plan on joining the Inc 500 this year?

6. **A set of Dumbo elephant ears.** It pains me to suggest that, as a rule, small business owners in general are not good listeners. We tend to listen with our mouths open and lips moving. The Dumbo ears, strategically positioned in our office, will remind us to make better use of our ears and less of our lips. Steven Covey said it best when he suggested that we should "Seek first to understand and then to be understood."

7. **Walking shoes.** We are spending way too much time behind our desks wading through endless streams of electronic mail. Tom Peters prescribed many years ago that the best leaders should "MBWA" (manage by walking around). Set aside a certain period of time each day just to walk around your office, sales floor, or factory and see what's going on. This can send a very powerful message to the troops. It shows you are sincerely interested in their work, and can open up lines of communication that otherwise may never open.

8. **A picture frame.** Find a picture that best illustrates your passion outside of work, insert it into this frame, and place this picture in a very conspicuous position in your office. This is a reminder that there is life outside of the office. It may be a picture of your family, the 18th hole at your favorite golf course, or your Harley.

9. **Personal note cards.** When was the last time you sent a personal thank you note to a customer? An employee? A supplier? We have become much too comfortable with electronic messaging and have forgotten the power of a personal touch. I know some CEOs that make a habit of sending at least one personal note a week to a key business stakeholder.

10. I have saved the best gift idea for last. It's a **gift certificate** to you, in fact. You fill in the amount and the store of choice. Why? You have worked very hard this year under very difficult economic conditions. While recognizing all of your employees' efforts this year, you may have overlooked the highest performer of all… yourself. Hence, treat yourself to something nice. You've earned it. FYI… next year will be no easier.

Happy Holidays.

Join Your Local Junto

January 2004

I have been reading a recent biography on Benjamin Franklin written by Walter Isaacson. It's a fascinating book about one of America's first great entrepreneurs. I believe what has interested me most about this book is that Franklin and I share two passions: *entrepreneurship and networking.*

Like many contemporary entrepreneurs, Franklin began working as an early teen. With each job he took on greater responsibility and a willingness to lead. As a printer, Franklin became the first person in America to manufacture type. Ben Franklin started his own printing business at the ripe age of 22, and the business grew rapidly. As time passed he became involved in a number of additional entrepreneurial endeavors including publishing, writing, newspapers, and the postal service.

According to Isaacson, Ben Franklin was a consummate networker. In 1727, about the same time he started his first business, Franklin organized a club of young merchants and called it the *Junto.* The small club consisted of enterprising tradesmen, artisans, and young working men. Initially, they met at a local tavern on Friday nights. Isaacson describes these meetings as follows: "They discussed issues of the day, debated philosophical topics, devised schemes for self-improvement, and formed a network for the furtherance of their own careers."

Within a short period of time, Franklin's *Junto* became so popular that he encouraged members to start their own groups. As a result, affiliate groups sprung up throughout colonial America. Historians believe that the *Junto* was the start of modern day service groups such as Rotary Clubs and Kiwanis, business groups such as a local Chamber of Commerce or a Vistage group, and professional business associations such as the National Realtors or the Screen

Actors Guild. Joining a similar group has almost become an American way of life for many business owners.

What motivated Franklin to start and then remain active in the *Junto* for most of his life? While the book does not go into great detail, my sense is that it was the same motivation that causes many business owners and leaders to join today's groups. These reasons include:

• **Brand Awareness.** Franklin was very conscious of his "brand" as an entrepreneur, a scientist, and a politician in Philadelphia and around the world. He saw the *Junto* as a great opportunity to promote himself and his business in the business community. Franklin also understood a key fact about marketing. That is, you either build your own personal brand, or you get branded. Being a member of his *Junto* helped Franklin begin to build a very positive image of himself in the business community.

• **Building Contacts.** Franklin loved to network and was always looking for ways to expand his personal and professional network of contacts. Part of the agenda for the weekly *Junto* meetings included a discussion of newcomers to the Philadelphia community and also newly opened businesses. The group even worked to connect members with others outside the group. Franklin would often ask, "Is there any man whose friendship you want and which the *Junto* or any of them can procure for you?" While the technology for building and managing contacts has changed dramatically in today's business groups, the aim has remained the same. As a member of a business group, today's business owners use contacts to find customers, employees, suppliers, and business partners.

• **Giving Back.** Ben Franklin was very grateful for the help that he received from his peers as a young man getting started in business. As he grew older and his business prospered, he saw the *Junto* as a means for helping other young entrepreneurs get started. He shared his experiences and best practices just as business owners do today at meetings, trade shows, and conferences.

• **Professional and Personal Growth.** Early in the development of the *Junto* Franklin created a guide for group discussion. This guide included 24 questions. Many of the questions were aimed at helping the members become smarter and better at what they did inside and outside of their respective businesses. Examples included: "Hath any citizen in your knowledge failed in his business lately, and what have you heard of the cause?" or "Have you lately heard of any citizens thriving well, and by what means?" Small business owners today seek similar learning opportunities. They attend group meetings and listen to speakers, share best practices, and exchange new ideas.

- **Relieve Isolation.** Ben Franklin was not one to stay isolated in his printing shop all day. He enjoyed attending meetings as a means of alleviating the crippling sense of isolation that many business owners felt then and continue to feel today. Whether it is a *Junto* or a local Vistage group, CEOs of businesses crave companionship and enjoy the company of their peers.

As you are writing or refining your New Year's resolutions for 2004, I recommend that you start or join a *Junto* of your own this year. If you are already involved in such a group, ask yourself how you can better that organization and hence improve your own position at the same time. My goal is to be active in three groups this year. It's comforting to know that I am following in the footsteps of such a great American patriot and an entrepreneurial icon as well.

*"It's never too late to learn,
but sometimes it's too early."*

~ CHARLIE BROWN, CARTOON CHARACTER

Have You Crossed the Line?

February 2004

My Vistage speaker this past month was Harvin Moore. The topic was business ethics. This topic is like cough medicine. You know you need to take it and you also know it may not taste very good. To my surprise, I not only enjoyed the presentation, but it "tasted good" as well.

Harvin Moore was a very successful businessman in Houston, Texas in the 1980s. He was a real estate developer, an attorney, and a banker. He combined each of these entities very nicely into a business conglomerate that earned him much recognition amongst his peers in Houston, and considerable financial gain as well. He seemed to have the Midas touch when it came to business.

In the mid-1980s the Savings and Loan crash rocked the financial and real estate industries and Moore's business was no exception. While his bank was still solvent there was enormous pressure to generate cash from their asset holdings. As a result the bank made several loans that included conditions of the borrowers. This violated federal banking regulations. As Harvin admitted to the group, he crossed the line when he made those loans.

Shortly after that time, the bank was audited and these questionable loans were discovered. Within months a federal grand jury indicted Moore for bank fraud. Rather than fight the charges in a very anti-banking environment, he pleaded guilty to the felony charges and spent over two years in a federal prison in Texas. In addition, he paid a substantial six-figure fine, lost his right to practice law, and his wife divorced him. In a very short period of time Moore went from being a multi-millionaire CEO to earning 17 cents an hour in the prison cafeteria.

This tragic story really caused me to consider what it means to "cross the line." As business owners we are faced with daily decisions that challenge our ethical values. Maybe it's taking advantage of an unknowing customer. Or possibly it's mistreatment of an employee. Misleading a vendor. Misrepresenting information to our bank. Funneling precious resources from the business into our own personal means. The list goes on. How do we decide when, where, and how to "cross the line?"

In Harvin Moore's case, his actions, by his own admission, were both illegal and unethical. However, at the time he felt the necessity to take these actions for the well-being of his business and its stakeholders. Would you have acted in a similar fashion?

I learned an important lesson for myself about business ethics early on in my entrepreneurial career. I was the owner and operator of a small retail business. Primarily for accounting purposes, I had multiple bank accounts set up. As money came in from customers, funds flowed from one account to another. As a sharp recent MBA graduate I began to become creative with these bank transfers when funds were low. I would write checks to transfer funds before the funds were actually available, knowing that before the check would clear, the necessary funds would be properly deposited. On occasion I would get caught short-handed and would pay a bounced check bank fee.

One day I got a call from my typically friendly banker. He asked me to come pay him a visit as soon as possible. That afternoon I went to his office. He was not happy. The bank had been keeping track of my creative funding and had decided it was time to put a halt to it. My banker informed me that I was guilty of check kiting and that this was a federal offense. If it continued they would close my accounts, call my loans, and prosecute if necessary. This was a wake-up call. I had not received a call like this in a very long time. There had never really been a discussion on business ethics in business school.

What I had perceived as creative financing, the bank had perceived as a felony. I had crossed the line and didn't know it. Under different circumstances and with larger dollar amounts, I, too, could have possibly been exposed to our federal judiciary and penal system.

The lesson for me in this experience was to scrutinize my decisions and my actions much closer prior to taking action. Otherwise that one action could easily become a norm or a habit. By waiting, it becomes much too easy to justify or legitimize our sometimes-desperate actions.

Luckily, about that same time in my entrepreneurial career, I found a book that helped me greatly in making tough ethical business decisions.

The book is *The Power of Ethical Management,* and best-selling author Ken Blanchard wrote it.

Blanchard recommends that you ask yourself three questions when faced with a tough decision. They are as follows:

- "Is it legal?"

- "Is it balanced?"

- "How will it make me feel about myself?"

If the answer to the first question is no, there is no reason to go to the second and third questions. The second question makes sure that your decision is a win/win for all parties concerned and that your gain is not a result of someone else's loss. The third question forces you to look in the mirror and make sure you can face yourself as a result of your decision.

These three questions have become a simple, yet powerful, filter for me as I have wrestled with tough ethical decisions in my business and personal life for over twenty years. They also serve as speed bumps for me. Sometimes I want to race and make quick decisions. However, they may have significant long-term ramifications for me and others involved. I am forced to slow down and sometimes stop to consider the possible outcome of my decisions.

Harvin Moore crossed the line and paid dearly. I have crossed the line on numerous occasions and have also paid the price. I hope that the next time you near "the line" you will think of Harvin. Consider the price you may pay. Ask yourself Blanchard's three questions and then be at peace with your decisions.

"Sometimes the questions are complicated and the answers are simple."

~ Dr. Seuss

Are You a Designer?

March 2004

Small business owners typically assume a variety of job titles, including chief marketing officer, chief financial officer, human resource manager, and operations manager, just to name a few. The following story caused me to think that there may be an additional job title inherent in being the business owner.

> A premier sculling coach took his team to a race. After weeks of practice and preparation, they lost. They returned home and the coach decided they needed to practice harder. So they did.
>
> The next race came, and they lost again. This time the coach decided they needed their morale lifted; so he threw a party and let them have the day off. At the next race, they lost.
>
> This cycle continued until the coach became so frustrated he decided he had lost his touch. Maybe it was time for him to retire. In desperation, he had the boat removed from the water so he could examine it.
>
> Once the boat was removed from the water, the problem became clear. The boat had been poorly constructed and was producing a strong drag on its forward movement. The team had been trying to win a race in a SQUARE boat.

Small business owners and operators, like the coach, easily forget that their job includes hull design and redesign. When looking for solutions to problems, it is usually easier to blame employees' work, attitudes, morale or even leadership than it is to ask fundamental questions about the design of the vehicles of our work. We forget to examine the *design* of the ship.

Sales and marketing guru Max Carey suggests that, "Your business is functioning exactly as it is designed to function." Like the coach, Carey says that we must first examine the current design of our business. While we might be tempted to start addressing employee and leadership behaviors, he states: "First, change the design of your company, then change your behavior."

The best athletes in the world won't win the race in a square boat. Nor will the best employees perform at their peak operating level with outdated, ineffective procedures, policies, and systems.

You don't have to be able to build the ship, but you must be able to examine and re-examine its effectiveness as if you had designed it yourself. It is important to not only have the ability to recognize a faulty design, but the willingness to do something about it. Recognition of the problem is the first step, but without rebuilding the hull, the coach is still left with a square boat.

I hope that your business enjoys smooth sailing this month....

"To create, you must first destroy."

~ PICASSO

It's Time to Keep Score of Your Business

June 2004

I enjoy playing golf but it can be a very frustrating game. For that reason, I typically do not keep score when I play golf. I find that it makes the game more enjoyable when I leave the scorecard and the half-pencil in the clubhouse. I have also found that, over the past three decades that I have played golf, my game has not improved at all. If anything, it has deteriorated over this time period. Then again it is hard to tell because... *I don't keep score.*

Many small business owners manage their business just like I play golf. They don't keep score. Their reasoning is very similar to mine as well. They say it just makes running their small enterprise that much more frustrating if they must look at monthly financial statements or weekly sales reports. In addition, since they work in the business every day, they know how the business is doing. What other information could they possibly need?

When friends ask what I normally shoot when I play golf, I usually respond with: "mid-nineties." That sounds pretty good and it seems about right. The funny thing is that when I do actually keep score, I usually shoot in the high-nineties and low-hundreds. In other words, I don't score as well as I presume I do.

Many small business owners think the same way. When I ask the business owner questions about profit margins, sales figures, or specific ratios, I will either get a blank stare (bad sign) or a rough estimate. Upon examining their financial statements, I usually find that their "rough estimates" are overstated, sometimes dramatically.

I tell small business owners the question is not whether or *not* they should be keeping score of their business. What they are operating is not a leisurely walk in the park slapping a silly white ball from tee to green. This is their livelihood. This is their dream. This is their business.

Instead, I inform them that the key question *is* what to keep score of. What should they be measuring and monitoring on a regular basis? How can they keep a pulse of their business on a day-to-day basis?

My dad was an entrepreneur. He was not the owner of the business but he had to think like an owner. He was in charge of operating a large warehouse distribution center. I can remember being in his office and always seeing a small piece of notepaper (this was before Post-its) in the upper front corner of his desk. Scribbled on that piece of paper were three numbers. On one occasion I asked my dad what those numbers were. Little did I know at that time that I was about to receive one of the best business management lessons I would ever receive, in or out of business school.

My dad responded that his bookkeeper brought him this sheet of paper every day with three numbers written on it. The numbers included the previous day's total sales, the current day's bank deposit, and the amount of outstanding accounts receivable on that particular day. He explained to me that those three numbers gave him the "pulse" of the business each and every day. This is how he kept score of his business. Through his experience in managing this business, he knew what to look for in these numbers. He knew what was "below-par, par, and above-par." He knew when his business "game" was on and when it was off. No guesswork there.

No one day's number would cause a panic. He was more concerned with patterns. Were sales increasing? Were receivables under control? He had a mental chart of each of these figures and would take action when necessary.

In addition to these daily reports, he would also receive weekly sales and inventory reports. He paid close attention to the monthly financial statements when they arrived. However, the daily reports were what he relied on most, and they allowed him to best keep score of his business. They were timely. They were accurate. They were critical to his ability to successfully manage the multi-million dollar operation.

What numbers should you be receiving every day? You decide. Possibilities include sales figures, bank deposits, inventory levels, employee timesheets, production reports, accounts receivable, accounts payable, and profit margins. Every industry has different areas of performance that need to be looked at regularly.

I think three is the magic number. Pick any three of these numbers and watch them every single working day. That is your mini-report card for the day. That is your scorecard. Set reasonable standards for each figure and be prepared to take action when necessary.

Keep score of your business and watch it improve and grow.

*"How did you go bankrupt? Very slowly…
and then all of a sudden."*

~ ERNEST HEMMINGWAY

IT'S A FUNNY WORLD

July 2004

(Warning: this article is not business-related, and, at best, may cause you to smile at some point while reading it.)

Sometimes the greatest gifts we receive in life come from the most unlikely places. I received such a gift recently, and I would like to pass it on.

One of my New Year's objectives for 2004 was to take two classes that were not directly business-related. In the spring I received the schedule of classes from Emory at Night, and glossed over the offerings. Most of the classes, such as square dancing, yoga, and middle-eastern cooking, just didn't grab my interest. Then I noticed a class description for a comedy writing class. The instructor was Brian Dycus, a local comedian and comedy writer. Although I have done a lot of writing in my career, I have never had any formal writing instruction since the nightmarish experience I had in my college freshman English class. On a whim I registered for the class.

During the first night of class we received our syllabus for the program. It was six weeks of learning about different formats of comedy and the different structures of comedy writing. It all looked very interesting. Then came the bombshell. Our graduation requirement was to write and perform approximately five minutes of live comedy in an open-mike format at a local Atlanta club in front of a live audience. It was clear that I had signed up for the wrong class. I must have made a mistake….

Our instructor then went to great lengths to assure us that this would not be an insurmountable task. Others before us had taken the class, performed their five minutes, and survived to talk about it. We would be no different. Reluctantly, I decided to stay in the class. That was one of my better decisions.

One of the first and most important lessons we learned was where and how to find humor. We learned there is humor all around us. We just have to know where to find it. We were instructed to look at almost any situation and ask the question, "What's funny about this?" Inevitably, we would find humor in just about every aspect of life. We explored our family relationships, to politics, to our own personal idiosyncrasies. By the end of the class, one couldn't help but believe that we live in a very funny world. This was a very different perspective than I had before taking the class.

The gift of humor is an extraordinary present. To see humor where I didn't see it before and help others laugh is a gift so precious that no dollar value could possibly be assigned to it. I now look for, and see, humor in places where I never thought I would ever find it, such as in grocery stores, driving on I-285, and in fierce conversations with my two sons. This newfound sense of humor has created a better mental balance in me as I wrestle with the pressures and stress of a busy work life.

I have also come to realize that many business owners don't have this same gift. It appears they almost seem to go to great lengths not to laugh while on the job. They find it almost impossible to find humor in their work and so they are quite serious all the time. What a painful experience this must be.

Before I knew it, the class had ended and my graduation performance had come. There were close to 150 people in the audience and the spotlight was so bright I could just barely see the shapes of heads in the front row. My topics included dieting, exercise, my work with CEOs, and date nights. The crowd laughed politely as I worked my way through the material. Some jokes got more laughter than others. I was actually having fun making others laugh. The time seemed to fly by.

My best laugh came at the end of the show as I headed toward the exit, and a younger member of the audience approached me and said, "Man, you were a lot funnier than I thought you would be." Now that was funny.

Your assignment: Over the next week take time at least once a day to stop and ask the question, *"What's funny about this?"*

"Laughter is inner jogging."

~ NORMAN COUSINS

How to Work on Your Business like a Jigsaw Puzzle

January 2005

I love working on jigsaw puzzles. Every year at the top of my Christmas wish list is a jigsaw puzzle. I will then spend a good part of the remaining holiday season and sometimes months into the next year working on that puzzle. I will spend hours at a time attempting to fit these puzzle pieces together into larger pieces that eventually all come together as one big completed puzzle. My family knows not to bother me when I am working on the puzzle, so they won't disturb my concentration. It is as if I am working on something far more important.

I have often wondered why I suffer from this infatuation with jigsaw puzzles. I have come to the conclusion that it may be the entrepreneurial spirit in me that rejoices at the notion of starting and finishing another puzzle. In fact, it has occurred to me that working on a jigsaw puzzle is a very similar process to that of working on a small business. In that respect, here are five steps to help you work on your very own jigsaw puzzle.

Step #1: Start with the end in mind.

This is hardly an original thought. It's one of Steven Covey's "Seven Habits." When I first start on a new puzzle I spend several moments staring at the box cover that shows the picture of the final puzzle. I try to create, in my own mind, the image of the final picture.

Successful entrepreneurs do the same thing with their respective businesses. They imagine what the business will look like when it's done or at the height of incredible success. This vision may include their customers, their employees, revenues, profitability, and more. Michael Gerber, in his best-selling book, *The*

E Myth, took this step a bit further. He suggested that you should imagine your business when you have ten thousand locations or something relatively comparable, and then plan accordingly.

Step #2: Make your work public.

I typically have my puzzle set up on the dining room table. It is very visible to everyone in my household. My family can check the status of my work at any time and I receive a lot of free consultation. Even our cat, Pepper, will saunter by on occasion and offer her quiet approval of my work. Friends and houseguests will see the puzzle and immediately take interest in my progress. As I make my work public, the project goes from my puzzle to our puzzle. The whole family takes some level of ownership in this project.

I have noticed that successful CEOs do the same thing. They are very good at making their work public. They share their plans with their employees. There are few secrets. While that may expose them to the opinions of their peers, the result is a much higher level of buy-in to their work and the direction of the organization.

Step #3: Start simple.

I always start by assembling the border of the puzzle. For me, the border pieces are the easiest pieces to find and put together. I am able to enjoy some level of success early in my work, as I am busy piecing together the border. In addition, when the border is done, I then have a visual representation of the boundaries of the puzzle, and it is very helpful.

I have found this step also works well when working on business projects. Some are very complicated. I try to start with the simple stuff. I gain confidence and then move on to the more difficult steps of the project. Establishing the boundaries for the project early on can also be very helpful.

Step #4: Stay organized.

After the border is done, I will gather half a dozen empty box covers and use them to organize the remaining pieces into groups. They may be grouped by colors, shapes, sizes, etc. Trying to work on one thousand puzzle pieces at one time can be quite overwhelming, therefore I try to break the pieces into these subgroups. Divide and conquer.

Businesses are organized the same way. Some are grouped by functional areas: marketing, finance, etc. Others may be organized by regions or by customer groups. Too many small boxes of puzzle pieces can be just as frustrating as having too many departments in a small business. I merge and combine boxes of puzzle pieces as needed. Small businesses need to be flexible, too.

Step #5: Be prepared for the unexpected.

Last night my wife decided she wanted to use the dining room for something other than working on my puzzle... like dinner. I was not prepared for this sudden turn in events. I had to enlist the help of my son to move the entire puzzle to my office without jarring a single piece.

A week ago, my soon to be someone else's house cat, Pepper, ventured into the dining room and plopped herself right on top of the puzzle as if it was her puzzle. This was a hostile takeover like none I had experienced before. She then proceeded to carefully shove several boxes of puzzle pieces to the floor. Finally, this insane cat began to rearrange the remaining puzzle pieces in an order that did not resemble my vision of the puzzle or that of the box cover. Fortunately, acting like a white knight, I dashed from my home office to the adjacent dining room in time to save the puzzle.

As a small business owner, can you imagine experiencing such chaos in your own business? How well do you manage such adversity?

I am currently about halfway done with my puzzle. It is a *Saturday Evening Post* magazine cover by Norman Rockwell. It is a very difficult puzzle. The pieces don't seem to fit together like they should and I seem to be missing several key pieces. I am also finding that I just don't have the time to work on the puzzle as much as I would like to. Does this remind you of anything?

Here is a final note about jigsaw puzzles. Like life, when I am done, all of the pieces go back into the box. Now, where's that cat?

> *"Man cannot discover new oceans unless he has the courage to lose sight of the shore."*
>
> ~ ANDRE GID

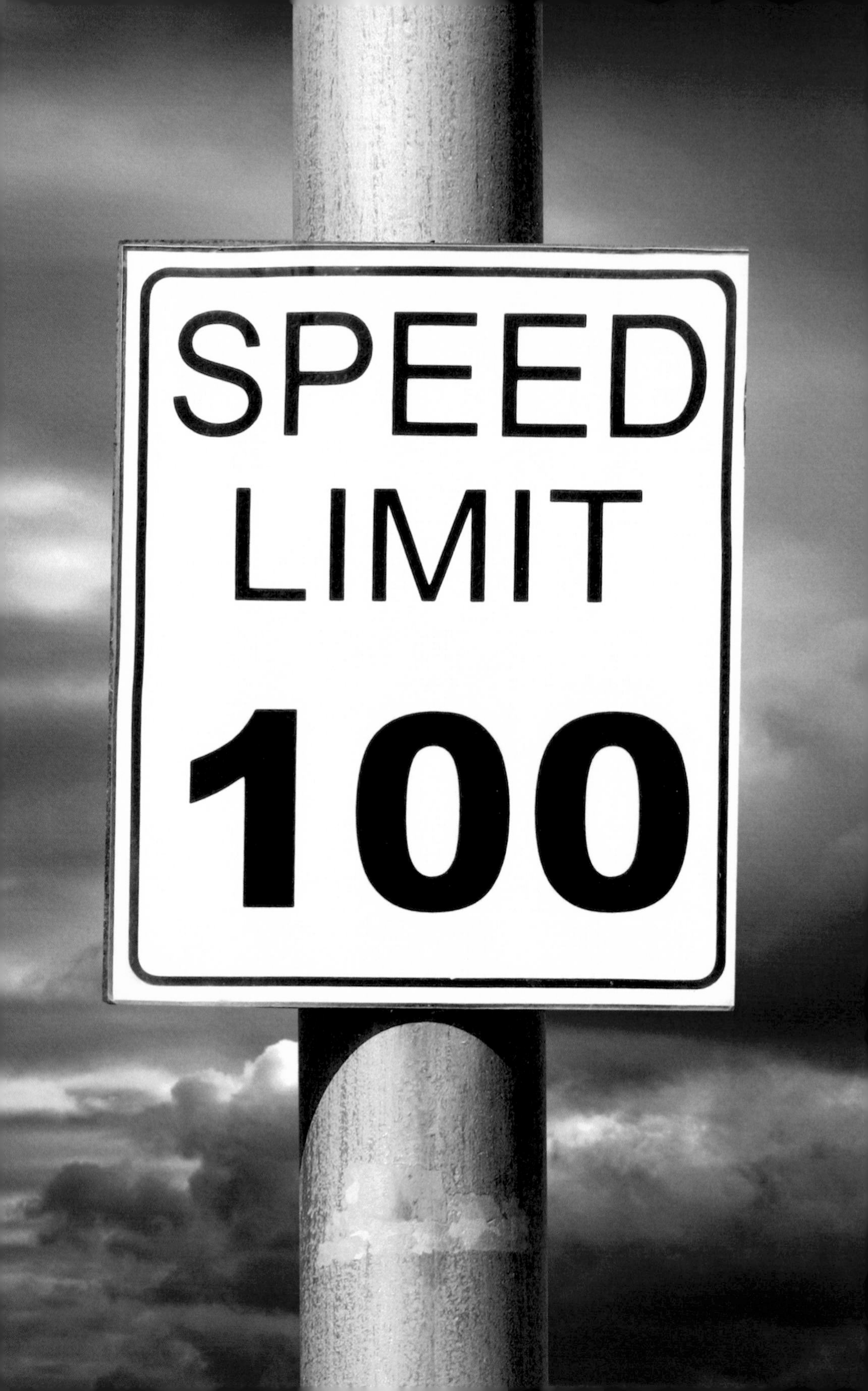
SPEED
LIMIT
100

What is your Business's Speed Limit?

May 2005

My wife and I have been married for over 23 years. As you might imagine, we agree far more than we disagree. One area of continual disagreement over time has been my driving. My wife suggests, unsolicited most of the time, that I drive too fast. Whether it's in my own neighborhood or on the interstate, she will politely communicate "SLOW DOWN!"

Hence, we will then debate the appropriate speed limit for that particular stretch of road. She will often suggest the speed limit posted by the road sign. I consider the sign to be an advisement of sort, and believe that the speed limit should be more of a combination of road conditions, traffic, and my own personal sense of urgency in arriving to my destination on time.

Often I find that there is a similar disagreement between business owners. How fast should I grow this business? Some business owners are very conservative in their judgment about growth. They are quite comfortable with slow or moderate growth, sometimes almost coasting their business vehicle with minimal effort.

Other small business owners go way too fast. They are like the drivers that lap me on I-285 on my way to the airport. They drive recklessly, with little consideration for their own personal welfare, that of their passengers, or other drivers. These are the same drivers I often see later on, pulled over by a state trooper or part of a multi-car crash on the side of the highway.

As a driver, I rely on my own intuition and some government regulation to determine how fast to drive my car. How do business owners make this same determination? I believe it is based on the following several factors.

Experience. A lack of entrepreneurial experience might cause a business owner to either grow the business too fast or too slow. Since they have not managed a business before, they don't know what a comfortable growth rate might be. Hence, they might harness the growth of the business as a result of this relative inexperience, or might push too hard for growth and then find themselves either crashing the business or running out of resources (fuel) prematurely.

My son is a relatively new driver. At times when I am driving with him I find myself politely suggesting to him to either speed up (infrequently) or slow down (more often). I am sometimes at a loss to explain my rationale to him, because it is often just a gut feeling based on my own driving experience.

Genetics. I honestly believe that some people are just wired internally to go faster than others. That's my excuse. I like to drive fast. My wife prefers a slow crawl (just kidding honey). Business owners are the same way. Some just have a greater tolerance for risk and are quite comfortable growing their business at a pace that would give others heart failure. While these business owners are not blind to the pitfalls of hyper growth, they are confident they can overcome these obstacles and still maintain rapid growth.

These "drivers" remind me of one of my favorite quotes: "Fixing a small business is like changing a flat tire on a car… at sixty miles an hour."

Availability of Resources. While I might like to be able to drive 75 mph on Ga 400, it is difficult to do that if I run out of gas, have bald tires, or faulty brakes. My car needs to be in good working order to support my "need for speed." Business owners are the same way. In order to support their growth needs they need adequate financial capital, capable employees, ample office space, and a variety of other corporate resources. A shortage of any one of these resources can severely restrict the growth aspirations of any business owner.

As a college sophomore I learned an important lesson about speed and taking care of my vehicle. I was on Thanksgiving break and was racing to get to Florida. In between Tallahassee and Ocala on I-10 my temperature light went on. I ignored it, assuming it was some type of electrical malfunction. Finally I stopped and just filled my radiator with water. Shortly after getting back on the road, the car severely overheated. I ended up doing irreparable damage to the engine, which then had to be replaced. This was a very costly mistake. How do you gauge whether your business engine is overheated or not?

External Factors. I do drive slower in the rain. I also slow down in heavy traffic. The road leading out of our subdivision has speed bumps so I am forced to alter my driving as a result of those impediments. There are certain market conditions that will cause business owners to slow down their growth rates too. A lagging economy or rising interest rates will curb growth. Stiff competition might alter growth plans. Government policies on trade or taxes might also impede corporate growth.

So what is a safe growth rate for a small business? If you assume that safety and risk are related, then a safe growth rate might be one that causes no undue risk to the business entity. Typically in business we evaluate risk in terms of the amount of debt or liabilities the firm has. Hence a safe growth rate is one that does not cause the firm to add undue risk or debt to its balance sheet. Here is a formula for calculating a sustainable growth rate taking this into consideration:

$$\text{Formula:} \qquad \frac{(\text{Net Profit\%}) \times (1 + \text{Debt/Equity})}{(\text{Var. Assets\%}) - [\text{NPM\%}) \times (1 + \text{Debt/Equity})]}$$

Let's assume the following: a firm has a 10% net profit margin, a debt to equity ratio of 50%, and a ratio of variable assets to total assets of 75%. What is their sustainable growth rate (SGR)?

$$\text{SGR} = \frac{(.10) \times (1 + .5)}{(.75) - (.10) \times (1 + .5)}$$

$$= .15/.6 = .25 \text{ or } 25\%$$

In this example, the firm can safely grow revenues at a rate up to 25% without assuming any additional relative debt (risk). If the firm wants to grow at a faster pace, it would have to increase its debt/equity ratio, thus increasing its risk factor. In addition, the business owner can also increase their sustainable growth rate by either improving their net profit margin or decreasing its use of variable assets as a percentage of total assets.

Using this equation, what is your company's sustainable growth rate?

In the last three years I have been in three auto accidents. In each case the other driver was at fault. Nevertheless I find myself driving slower these days. Why take a chance with #4? I suggest you do the same with your business. Watch the speed limit.

"*The important thing is to win at the slowest speed possible.*"

~ Johnny Rutherford, race car driver

THE PERFECT BUSINESS?

July 2005

Imagine the perfect small business. What comes to mind? How about the following?

• Customers are willing to pay 3–5 times the retail price for your goods or services.

• Customers are willing to make significant sacrifices to come to your place of business, sometimes traveling overnight. Most customers arrive early, sometimes hours before you open.

• Customers applaud your employees' efforts. There are frequent standing ovations despite the fact that, in almost a century as a business, you have only had one great year.

• Your product has been sold out for the past two years and will continue to be for years to come.

• You have a monopoly in your market. No other direct competitor may open a similar business in your metropolitan area.

Is this make-believe? No. This small business is the Boston Red Sox, a Major League Baseball franchise.

This past weekend I had the incredible opportunity to travel to Boston and attend two Red Sox games with my oldest son. They played their arch nemesis the New York Yankees. For two raving baseball fans, this was a most memorable experience. Fenway Park, where the Red Sox play their home games, is almost one hundred years old, and is a mecca for our national pastime. The stadium is archaic when compared to many of today's modern baseball facilities such as Turner Field. There is no Jumbotron screen in centerfield, no amusement park for the kids to play in, and no concert-like sound system booming Aerosmith with each player introduction. You see very few cell phones, few corporations entertaining clients, and no empty seats.

We arrived at the stadium at 11 a.m. for a 1 p.m. game on a Saturday. There were already thousands of fans in line waiting to enter the stadium. We did not have tickets for the game, and I began to search for someone with extra tickets to sell. Before leaving for the game in Boston I had tried to buy tickets via Ebay, and found no tickets for less than $200. I purchased tickets with a face value of $28 for $175 each. Why so much? The Red Sox had over 120 straight sold out games in Fenway Park.

As I sat during the game I couldn't help but think what a great business model this was. Wouldn't any small business owner desire to have such an incredibly successful enterprise? How have the Red Sox achieved such entrepreneurial stardom? Here are my own observations.

Shared Fate. Until last year's World Series win, the Red Sox and their fans had gone over 80 years without a title. Their fans and the team had suffered through several heartbreaking years when they came very close to a championship but fell short. Despite this string of failures, the team and their beloved fans had developed a strong bond of shared fate. They suffered together. True Red Sox fans never gave up on their team while, the team did what they could every year to build a winning team. *As a small business owner, how would you describe the shared fate you enjoy with your customers? How long would they be willing to put up with subpar performances before switching their allegiance to another "team" (competitor)?*

The Experience. Going to a Red Sox game at Fenway Park is not like going to just another baseball game. It is an experience that only a true baseball fan can relate to. It is a baseball "nirvana." The moment you enter this cathedral of sport you sense the history that has taken place there over the last century: World Series games, All-Star games, and historic individual performances. Visions of Red Sox greats such as Ted Williams, Carl Yastrzemski, and even Babe Ruth can be seen rounding the bases. It could just as easily be 1945 instead of the year 2005 and you sense that nothing would be different. As a customer, I expect more than just an exchange of goods and services from a business provider. I expect to be rewarded. In this case I was rewarded with a very competitive game, in a world-class arena, and a memory of an experience with my son that will last forever. *What type of experience does your customer get when they come to your place of business? What type of reward do they earn as a result of doing business with you?*

It's Not About the Price. While the Red Sox do not have any direct competition from other professional baseball teams in the Boston area, there is no shortage of other entertainment venues in Boston. One can choose from a variety of other sporting events, concerts, shows, museums, and other types of entertainment. Why is it that this team can charge such a premium for game tickets? Why is it that fans like me are willing to pay such high multiples to attend a game? I believe it's about value. It's almost impossible to justify paying $175 to sit on a hard bleacher seat in hot summer weather for three hours, other than to say assigning a price to the value I received from this experience is very difficult. As the MasterCard commercials suggest… "it's priceless." *How many of your customers feel this way about your product or service? How many of them are willing and able to write you a blank check just so they can do business with you?*

There may not be a perfect business, just as there may not be a perfect customer. I will continue to enjoy my journey looking for both. For a father and his son however, this was a perfect trip.

"Nobody succeeds beyond his or her wildest expectations unless he or she begins with wild expectations."

~ RALPH CHARELL

WHO IS YOUR MOST IMPROVED PLAYER (MIP)?

May 2006

My wife and I attended my oldest son Taylor's baseball banquet earlier this month. The team was much improved this year, so there was much anticipation about which players would earn recognition for their performance during the season. Taylor had a good season with a batting average just under 300 and had been one of the team's most consistent fielders while playing shortstop each game.

After dinner, the coach began to present the player awards. He recognized the best hitter, the best fielder, the player with the most spirit, the rookie of the year, the most valuable player, and several others. With each award I could sense that Taylor was becoming more and more anxious as he had not yet been recognized. Finally, the coach announced a new award: *Most Improved Player (MIP)*. This award would recognize the player who had made the most improvement from the previous year. He took what seemed like an eternity to describe the accomplishments of this player. He spoke with great pride about how this player had progressed from a part-time utility player the year before to a leader of the team this year. He spoke of a meeting in the beginning of the year when he challenged this player to establish himself as a starter on the team. Lastly, he spoke of how much he enjoyed working with this player and how much he would miss him, as he would be leaving the team as a graduating senior.

Finally, he announced the name of the recipient of the *Most Improved Player* award: Taylor Fulton. Our son stood slowly and with great pride moved to the podium to receive his award. Mom and Dad shared a glance that only parents can understand. Both of us did our best not to show the tears of happiness we shared while watching our son be recognized.

While Taylor would have been happy to receive any of the awards presented at the banquet, no award meant more to him than this one. No other award would have recognized the enormous amount of time and effort he invested in himself to prepare for this season. He was both pleasantly surprised and humbled by this recognition from his coach. He will remember this moment for the rest of his life. This was a life lesson about hard work and determination that could have never been learned in a classroom.

Several days after the banquet I began to wonder how many business owners recognize their MIPs. It's not unusual for a business to recognize their most valuable players from the CEO to the top sales representative. Many businesses also recognize top performers in terms of productivity, fewest errors, and best attendance. However, I can't ever remember hearing of any business recognizing their most improved employee. This would be the employee who had made the most improvement in their work performance within a certain time period.

As a result I urge you to consider the following questions:

• Who is your MIP?

• What have you done to recognize this person?

• What impact would recognizing this person have on their future performance?

• What impact would publicly recognizing this employee have on other employees who might not be performing at the highest level?

• How often should you recognize employee improvement?

• How should you recognize this person? Individually? In front of his peers?

I imagine among the group of players at the banquet there could have been an underclassman questioning whether it was worth the time and effort to improve their game to the next level for the upcoming season. It's possible that in seeing Taylor earn his recognition, an underclassman decided it was indeed worth his time. Hence, I believe there is a viral effect to recognition.

Taylor may never pick up a baseball bat or throw a baseball again. He has played the game for 12 years and has had a ball. College is his next "game" and I intend to monitor and reward his improvement there as well.

*"The best way to
keep a good employee
is to fire a bad one."*

~ BOB THOMPSON

Am I a Flashlight or a Hammer?

October 2006

Last week I was invited to speak to a Small Business Management class at Georgia State University. I always look forward to speaking to college classes, as I find they ask very tough questions and sometimes cause me to question my answers while I am answering their questions.

This class had been given an assignment by their professor. They were to find a small business and go fix it. During my presentation, one student asked me, "How do you go about fixing businesses?" I was prepared to give my standard answer to the question when it occurred to me that this was a good time for some brutal honesty.

"I don't fix businesses," I responded. A quiet hush fell over the classroom as I gave them an answer they did not expect.

"My job is like that of a flashlight," I continued. The look on their faces went from being curious to that of seeing the "emperor with no clothes." I went on to explain that my role as a consultant is to help the business owner shed light on their own problems, and then continue to help them determine the appropriate courses of action to address those problems. Finally, I hold them accountable for the execution of their intended strategy.

"Isn't it just easier for you to name the problem and then get them to pay you to fix it?" asked one student from the back of the room.

I responded, "It is easier, and the likelihood of that problem actually getting fixed is slim to none."

My own painful experience is that the business owner must take responsibility for their own problems before they are prepared to take action on them.

"Tell me more about this flashlight thing," asked another student.

"It all starts and ends with asking the right questions," I shared with the class.

"Couldn't they just ask themselves their own questions and save the expense of a high-priced consultant?" asked one student with a smile on his face.

"It's not that easy," I countered quickly. "They must be the right questions."

At that point, I proceeded to share with the group a short list of my favorite client questions. I was impressed that they were writing down my questions as quickly as I could state them. I have found stealing material to be the highest compliment to a business consultant. I was feeling very good at this point.

Here are the questions I offered to them:

How much time do you spend working in the business versus working on the business?

Author Michael Gerber suggests it should be a thoughtful balance between the two. Most small business owners find themselves working far too much in the business and not nearly enough time on the business.

What is your competitive advantage?

A competitive advantage is a core competency, unique to the market, which the client has a great need for. If your competitive advantage is your price, your product is a commodity and your future is bleak.

If you had unlimited cash, what would you do with it?

I get very interesting answers to this question. Examples typically include the purchase of equipment, real estate, or technology. I also often hear the desire to hire key employees like sales people or customer service reps. I have a follow-up question to this one: What are you waiting on? In most cases, the issue is not a lack of capital. It is a lack of confidence. Capital is relatively easy to find. Confidence is not.

What is your exit strategy?

"Begin with end in mind." This is one of Steven Covey's "habits" that drive both entrepreneurial and personal success. I believe that almost all tough business issues must be addressed within the context of the owner's exit strategy. If there is no such exit strategy, then the business strategy we formulate may either work in favor of, or in opposition to, the owner's ultimate, often ill-planned, exit.

What is your story?

Every business has a story. The story should involve drama and conflict. It should pit good versus evil. It is what drives employee motivation and hence behavior. If the story is one of optimism and hope, employees will respond favorably. If it is a story of confusion or despair, employees will react accordingly. I believe it is the business owner's responsibility to craft and then communicate the story. Key stakeholders need to be reminded of the story as frequently as possible.

What is the last thing you stopped doing?

This question is all about discipline. The discipline to say no just as often as we say yes is key. Business owners are typically very good at starting new initiatives and not very good at knowing when to stop old initiatives. Before I work with a client, I need to know they have such discipline.

How did you answer these questions? There are more that I like to ask, but these are a sampling of my favorites. When asking these questions, the "flashlight" gets brighter with each question. I can see more and more into the business with each response and so can the business owner. It's almost like solving a jigsaw puzzle. We piece together each response into a clearer and more definitive picture. By the time we are done, the spotlight shines directly on the issues that need to be addressed.

One student raised her hand and asked a final question. "These questions seem more like a hammer than a flashlight. Each question pounds the business owner harder and harder. How do they survive?" I had never considered myself the hammer before, but it was an interesting comparison. Maybe I should ask that of my next client.

Are you asking yourself the right questions?

"Judge a man by his questions rather than his answers."

~ VOLTAIRE

THE MYTHS AND REALITIES OF ENTREPRENEURSHIP

February 2007

I have spoken to, and worked with, thousands of small business owners. In doing so, I have found that there are a number of myths about entrepreneurship. Now is a good time to dispel these myths and discover the realities of starting and growing a small business.

Myth #1: Most small businesses are started by entrepreneurs.

Reality: Most small businesses (over 90%) are started by technicians. Michael Gerber in his best-selling book, The E Myth, describes technicians as individuals who have a particular technical skill, who then start a business that utilizes or sells that skill. Examples of technicians include the chef who opens a restaurant, the auto mechanic who opens a repair garage, and the doctor who opens a health practice. The true entrepreneur is a builder, a visionary, and a creator. The entrepreneur enjoys working as much *on* the business as he/she does working *in* the business.

Myth #2: It gets easier.

Reality: My experience is that owning a business never gets easier. You may enjoy it more over time. The issues may evolve from the more tactical to the more strategic as the business grows. It's not like riding a bike. If you do find it getting easier, you need to start finding challenges for yourself and your organization that will result in growth opportunities for both.

Myth #3: Market research is primarily for business start-ups and big companies.

Reality: Information is power. In some cases it is the small business's competitive advantage. Information comes from market research. You should be continually gathering data on your product offering, competitors, and customers. The marketplace is changing so fast, and is way too fluid to assume these three critical cornerstones of your business are not changing as well. Make a commitment to ongoing market research. Make sure that your firm has an efficient and cost-effective means of collecting and interpreting the data, and that you are prepared to take action on the information as needed.

Myth #4: Intelligence (IQ) is a primary indicator of entrepreneurial success.

Reality: It's hard to downplay the value of being a smart business owner. However, there are two other qualities that I think are of equal or greater importance. The first is your emotional intelligence, as measured by your Emotional Quotient (EQ). This calculates how well you relate to other people, including your employees, customers, and other organizational stakeholders. There have been a lot of studies done in the past decade on this topic. They clearly show how important EQ is, and the relative importance of this quality in terms of leadership. Maybe even more important is your Adversity Quotient (AQ). This measurement assesses your ability to overcome adversity in your business and personal life. The number of average daily adversities has doubled in the last five years. Successful entrepreneurs are able to overcome adversity on a daily basis and stay focused on the task(s) at hand. Their mindset at times is "this too shall pass."

Myth #5: The business owner's job is to cut costs.

Reality: Many business owners seem to have bought into this myth. Today's newspaper headlines are filled with stories of businesses announcing massive layoffs, closing manufacturing plants, and outsourcing internal work processes. Vistage speaker Jack Harms suggests that the business owner has a far greater task instead: raise prices. In fact, he suggests that each month this question should be asked: "What have I done this month to raise prices?" Why raise prices? The only way we can raise prices in the long run is to provide greater value to our customers. So the question really is: "What have I done this month to provide greater value for my customers?"

Myth #6: A business plan is primarily for a business start-up, or to raise capital for an existing business.

Reality: A good business plan should be your "road map" to success. It should clearly articulate the vision and direction of your business. The plan also ensures that your business has a design and a purpose built into it. It is very easy to get lost in the course of your business. The business plan helps you find your way. The plan can also act as a set of speed bumps when your business vehicle exceeds your natural growth speed. About 80% of all small businesses fail in 3–5 years. Over 80% of all small businesses lack a business plan. Is there a direct correlation? Maybe not, but it is too hard to ignore the relative coincidence. Remember, the greatest value of a business plan is found in the actual development of the plan, not so much in the document itself.

Myth #7: Financial reporting is for accountants and the IRS.

Reality: Financial reporting allows the business owner to "keep score" of his/her business. Running a business is a lot like playing most sports. Improvement only comes by tracking our performance. Imagine playing nine innings of baseball without being able to see a scoreboard or know the score. How would you know when to switch pitchers or pinch-hit batters? The most successful professional sports managers and coaches keep track of many important statistics. Entrepreneurs need to do the same. Determine which financial numbers (key indicators) you need to follow and then commit to tracking them regularly.

Have I left out any entrepreneurial myths that you have experienced? Please let me know. In the meantime, stay focused on the realities and continue to enjoy the dream of entrepreneurship.

"The most valuable 100 people to bring into a deteriorating society would not be 10 chemists, or politicians, or professors, or engineers, but rather 100 entrepreneurs."

~ ABRAHAM MASLOW

SIX ROLES OF THE CEO

May 2007

I was asked recently to describe the role of the Chief Executive Officer (CEO) of an organization. As I considered the question, I realized that there were at least six roles that came to mind. I am sure there are more. Here are the six roles of a CEO I described:

Casting Director

I believe that staffing a small business is like casting a movie or a play. No matter how good a screenplay is, if the cast is not strong, the production will be a flop. Small businesses are the same way. You can have a dynamite business plan, but it's the people who make it successful.

Jim Collins, author of *Good to Great*, said it best: "You must get the right people on the bus, wrong people off the bus, and the right people in the right seats." This may be the most important role of the CEO.

Scorekeeper

I attended my son's baseball game recently and encountered a very interesting, and frustrating, situation. The game had started, and it became apparent right away that nobody was operating the scoreboard. No record was being kept of the number of balls, strikes, runs scored, or outs in the innings. Initially, this did not seem to be a big deal. However, the game progressed, innings passed, and runs were scored. As spectators, we were totally in the dark. We didn't know who was winning or losing, what inning the game was in, or even what the batter's count was. The players were just as ignorant about the status of the game as we were. They depended on the scoreboard as much as we did. Where was the scorekeeper?

How many small businesses are run without a scorekeeper? I believe there are many. Employees work hard, just like the baseball players, never knowing the results of their efforts. Just as it doesn't make sense for the baseball scorekeeper to only keep score for himself, it also doesn't make sense for the business owner to keep his own score and not share the results with his key stakeholders.

Designer

I recall the story of the sculling coach whose team was unable to win any races, until he took time to lift the racing boat out of the water—then he discovered the boat had a fatal design flaw. I believe it is the role of the CEO to oversee the design of his/her business and then periodically make sure the design is reviewed and is still working.

Michael Gerber, author of the best-selling book, *The E Myth*, suggests that while designing our business we should assume it is the first of 10,000 locations. What does that mean? I interpret this to mean we should seek out a design that can be replicated. It should be one that ensures the highest level of consistency of performance. Gerber also suggests that we should design our business as if we were designing a game. The game has rules. There must be a way to win the game. The game must be fun. We shouldn't design a game for our employees if we are not prepared to play ourselves.

Chief Fun Officer (CFO)

Have you ever seen a business that was having fun, but was also very successful? I believe the two go hand in hand, and that ultimately the CEO is responsible for making that happen. Let me be clear: I do not believe that the CEO should do this at the expense of his ability to lead. The CEO does not need to also be the CEY (Chief Executive Yuckster), responsible for making everyone laugh.

The CEO should make sure employees have the opportunity for fun since it contributes to their performance. Examples of this might be celebrations (birthdays, anniversaries, etc.), toys in the workplace (ping-pong, foosball etc.), or just looking for opportunities to be light-hearted. Laughter or even a smile can do wonders in a high stress/high performance work environment.

Storyteller

Leadership guru and Vistage speaker Don Schminke shared a leadership model with one of my groups that really made sense to my members and me. He suggested the results we seek from our employees are a direct result of their work behavior. Their behavior is driven by their beliefs. Their beliefs are a result of the "story." What story you ask? The story of your business. A story exists in every business, and sometimes more than one exists. The story might be a positive one, resulting in great employee efforts for your organization, or the story may be one of doom and gloom, and then employee performance can suffer.

I believe that the CEO is responsible for developing the right story for their respective business, and then communicating the story at every opportunity. In fact, each CEO should have three stories to tell at any given moment: a story about the past, one about the current situation of the business, and, more importantly, a story about the future.

Consider this: As a young child, how did we learn about life? Most of us learned through stories. We learned from books and stories from our parents, grandparents, and friends. Those stories at an early age most certainly impacted our behavior then, and most likely continue to impact our lives as adults. Stories are very powerful communication tools.

Race car Driver

I believe so much of what a successful CEO does today is manage velocity. Customers want everything faster. The pace of business today is much quicker than ever before. Hence, the CEO needs to be able to accelerate his/her business accordingly. Vistage speaker Ole Carlsson suggests that, "The CEO must have his hand on the gear shift at all times, prepared to up shift or downshift at any given moment."

Likewise, the CEO must know when to pull his car over for a quick pit stop when necessary. That's when it is time to fuel up (cash infusion), check the tires (employee performance reviews or 121 meetings) and check under the hood (planning meeting). One speaker recently said, "Changing a business is like changing a flat tire on a car... doing 60 miles an hour." Not even a race car driver would attempt that feat.

What have I left out? I'm sure there are several more traditional CEO roles that you find yourself in at times. Which role are you most comfortable in? Which role are you most uncomfortable in? Which role is most needed in your organization today? Sometimes it's better to be asking the right questions than always looking for more answers.

"The credit belongs to the man who is actually in the arena, whose face is marred by dust and sweat and blood, who knows the enthusiasms, the great devotions, and spends himself in a worthy cause; who at best, if he wins, knows the thrills of high achievement, and, if he fails, at least fails daring greatly, so that his place shall never be with those cold and timid souls who know neither victory nor defeat."

~ Theodore Roosevelt

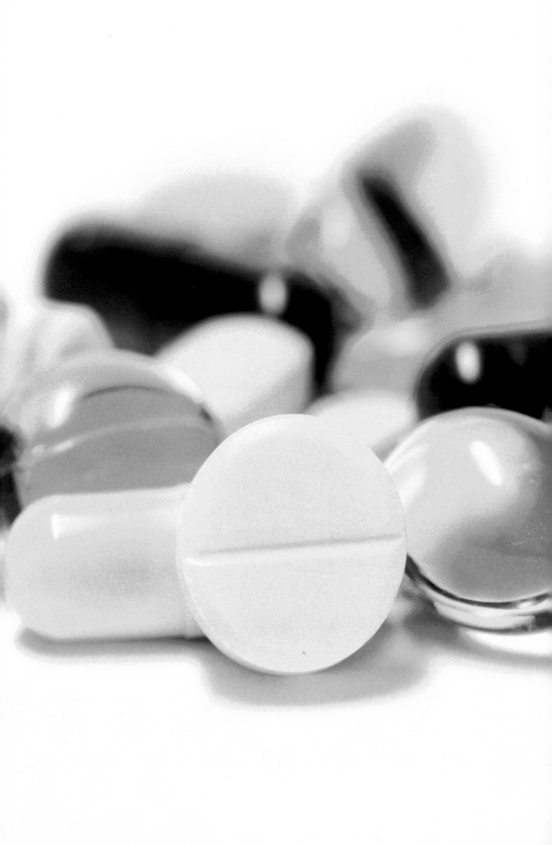

Are You Selling Aspirin or Vitamins?

July 2007

I have always been very interested in better understanding the mindset of the customer. In marketing terms, this area of study is known as psychographics. What motivates the buyer to purchase one product over another? Colgate over Palmolive? McDonald's over Burger King? Dell over Hewlett-Packard?

I believe at the end of the day all products and services fall into two broad categories—aspirin and vitamins. Let's examine the purchasing process for both of these generic products to better understand the buyer's mindset and decision-making process.

When I need to buy aspirin there are usually two concurrent events taking place in my life. First, I have a very bad headache. Second (and worse), there is not a single aspirin tablet to be found anywhere in my home. I check all of the kitchen drawers, the medicine cabinets, and even under the cushions on the living room couch. There is no aspirin anywhere. I am in great physical and emotional pain. The only solution is to get in my car, drive roughly three-fourths of a mile to the local convenience store, and buy some aspirin. At this point I am driving like a wild man. Thank goodness there weren't any pedestrians in the street.

When I arrive at the store I rush to the appropriate aisle where the aspirin is situated right next to the Fritos. I grab the first bottle of aspirin in sight and dash to the checkout line and wait for the guy buying lottery tickets to remember his favorite numbers. I throw twenty dollars at the less-than-friendly cashier, and dash back to my car with medication in hand. I rip the top off the bottle and down two or more tablets using two-day-old, warm, leftover sweet iced tea. The pain I feel begins to ease immediately.

My process for buying vitamins is very different. I will wait until my monthly visit to Costco to make this purchase. After purchasing several hundred dollars of items (much of which I am not sure what to do with) I come across the fifty-foot aisle of vitamins. I will take 20–30 minutes to study each option by carefully examining the quality of each product, the amount included, and, of course, the cost per tablet. I compare the branded products versus the generic products. I take notice of the shapes and sizes of each offering. After much deliberation, I make a decision and move on to the checkout line. I am impressed with myself on how diligent I have been in this purchase. I am feeling better already, despite not having taken a single pill.

So is there a difference between the two purchasing processes for both products? Of course there is. In the case of the aspirin my intent is to singlehandedly reduce or eliminate the *pain* I am experiencing. As for the vitamins, I am interested in *feeling better*. How do these different motivations impact my purchasing patterns? Do I care about price when buying aspirin? How important is ease of purchase (convenience) when buying vitamins?

Which product are you selling—aspirin or vitamins? More importantly, which product are your customers buying? Is it possible you are selling vitamins and your customers are buying aspirin? Is it possible that some of your customers are buying aspirin and others are buying vitamins?

My first business venture was an automotive tire and repair business. In most cases, the customers were buying aspirin. They would have a tire go bad so it needed replacing, or their car engine would be malfunctioning and need immediate repair. These were not happy customers. They did not choose to spend money on their car, but they were almost forced to. They were in pain and needed a quick resolution to their problems. Price was typically not an issue. Instead, the most common question was, "How long before it will be fixed?" These customers did not look forward to visiting my store. Our aim was to treat them fairly, fix the car right the first time, and minimize their respective downtime. I sold a lot of aspirin during this time and never knew it.

My second business was a travel agency. Our customers there were very different than the tire store customers. We were selling vitamins for the most part. Our clients traveled because they wanted to. They would come in the agency to plan exciting vacation getaways to faraway places. We were in the business of fulfilling dreams. Our customers scheduled their visits to our office. They would often have a budget to work from. They would study all of the travel brochures. Sometimes it would take months before they would finish planning their trips and make their final payments. We found that it was important for our agents to be very knowledgeable and patient when working with these clients. We sold a lot of vitamins in that business.

Once we collectively understood the mindset of our customers in each of these businesses we were in a much better position to better serve their needs. We also made better decisions on marketing to the customers. Certain types of marketing are better suited for selling aspirin than for vitamins. We also made better hiring decisions. Certain people are better at selling aspirin than selling vitamins. This research also helped us become more profitable, as we were able to build a financial model around each particular product.

I have often been asked before if I have a preference between selling aspirin or vitamins. My answer is no. Each of them has its advantages and disadvantages. The key, I believe, is to understand the difference between the two.

"Success isn't about being perceived as the best at what you do, it's about being perceived as the only one who does what you do."

~ JERRY GARCIA, GRATEFUL DEAD

TOP TEN SCARIEST MOMENTS
FOR A SMALL BUSINESS OWNER

October 2007

1. You receive an official letter from the Internal Revenue Service.

2. You notice a key employee surfing Monster.com.

3. Hiring your first key employee.

4. Firing your first key employee.

5. Your conversation with your CPA starts off with "I have good news and bad news...."

6. You receive an invitation to bid on an RFQ... from your best customer.

7. Your IT technician announces your systems will be down temporarily.

8. Firing your first customer.

9. You notice the business card of your top competitor on the desk of your best customer.

10. The thought of working for someone else....

Happy Halloween!

RECESSION? CHOOSE NOT TO PARTICIPATE.

January 2008

Listen to or read the news on any given day this month and I'll bet the lead story is about our declining economy. The housing market is falling. Unemployment is rising. Lowering interest rates. Weak dollar. More bankruptcies. Retail sales are down. Borrowing is up. Economists are beginning to use the dreaded "R" word (recession).

Where is the good news?

Here it is. As a small business owner you can still choose to not participate in this economic free-fall. That's right. You can exclude yourself from the pain and suffering others will be feeling if you act quickly. Instead, you can choose to outperform the market. If your industry is predicted to fall 10% this year, your goal may be to minimize that decline to 5%, or possibly just maintain your market share this year.

I firmly believe that you can choose the direction your business is going over the next couple years if you are proactive now.

Nationally recognized economist and Vistage speaker Brian Beaulieu suggests the following three strategies for small business owners facing an economic downturn:

#1: Accumulate cash. This is not a time to be investing a lot of your cash reserves in acquiring fixed assets such as land, buildings, or expensive equipment, for two reasons: First, they may be overpriced, as we are coming out of a strong economy which has inflated the value of such high-priced assets. Secondly, there are going to be great purchasing opportunities when the economy bottoms out. You will want to have currency available so you can take advantage of these low-priced deals.

How can you accumulate cash? Tighten your collection policies. Attempt to stretch your payables as much as possible. Negotiate the best terms possible from your vendors. Manage your inventory better. Liquidate any dead inventory that is not moving.

#2: "Get the right people on the bus and the wrong people off the bus." This quote comes from Jim Collin's book, Good To Great. Now is not the time to be carrying marginal performers on your payroll. I suggest you rank all of your employees from top to bottom, and force yourself to make a business case for why you are carrying the bottom quartile (25%). I don't believe that you can afford to carry these underachievers through two years of economic downturn.

Here are several specific strategies to address this issue:

- Consider moving as many of your employees to a "pay for performance" compensation model.

- Do you have any employees that might be interested in becoming independent contractors?

- Consider using temporary hires before making them permanent employees.

- Is there work that can be outsourced rather than using full-time employees?

#3: Be laser-focused in marketing to your target prospects. In good times, we may be able to market to wider target markets or use mass marketing strategies. In tight economies, we must narrow our marketing focus. Use the Pareto Principle (80-20). Generally speaking, 80% of your sales are coming from 20% of your customers. I suggest you focus on that 20%. How can you boost sales from those best customers?

Likewise, we cannot afford to focus our marketing efforts on too many different target markets. We need to be very precise in targeting just those few markets that will deliver the best return on investment from our scarce marketing resources. It's time to exercise our very best guerilla marketing tactics.

Here's the best news. If you are successful in outperforming a down market over the next two years, you will be very well positioned to take advantage of what will be a very strong recovery following the downturn. There are good times ahead, and you will be on the forefront of that tidal wave.

The time to act is now.

"Between stimulus and response, there is space.
In that space is our power to choose our response.
In our response lies our growth and our freedom."

~ VICTOR FRANKL

Life Lessons at Age 50

August 2008

I passed a big life milestone this month as I turned 50. I had several very nice surprises, including a dinner party with a number of out of town guests, and a visit from my son and his girlfriend from college. Turning 50 was not nearly as traumatic as I had anticipated a year ago when I started to prepare myself for hitting the half-century mark.

Living a half-century has afforded me the opportunity to learn several life lessons of which I took time to reflect upon this month. Each of these has impacted my life in a significant way. I share them with you in the hope that maybe they might impact you in a similar fashion.

1. I work to live.

For a good part of my life I am not sure this was the case. My life was work. I made great sacrifices in my life to improve my work. Today, I could stop working and I would be very happy. As I look toward the second half of my adult life, I look forward to working much less and spending more time with family, more time traveling, and more time sharpening my tennis skills.

2. At the end of the game, all of the pieces go back in the box.

I remember this moment like it was yesterday. It was two days after Hurricane Andrew in south Florida, and I was walking in my neighborhood in Homestead. The devastation was unbelievable. I was in a state of shock. Our home and business had been destroyed and our possessions had been blown to parts unknown. I ran into a very good friend of mine who had experienced similar losses. After we briefly compared notes on the damages we had both incurred, he shared the above statement with me for the first time. It really hit home quickly.

I was reminded of the many games of Monopoly I had played as a child. After hours of fierce competition, we would accumulate cash, houses, and even railroads. Ultimately, the game would end and all of the pieces would go back into the box. No one player was any better off for what they had accumulated during the game. It was just a game.

Leading up to Hurricane Andrew, I had focused much of my life accumulating a lot of "pieces." In a matter of minutes during the storm, many of those pieces returned back to the "box." Since that time, I have again accumulated a lot of pieces. Once again the pieces will go back in the box at some point in time.

3. God doesn't prevent the storms; He just helps us get through them.

This life lesson was also a result of my experience with Hurricane Andrew. In the aftermath of the disaster, my spiritual faith was tested in a way that I hope I don't face again in my lifetime. I could not understand how my Creator could allow such massive destruction and despair to occur.

Several weeks after the storm I attended church for the first time. The roof on the church had been ripped off during the storm and we had a direct view of the sky and the heavens above. The sermon that day seemed to be directed right at me, though I am sure that there were many others who were wrestling with this same spiritual dilemma. The message was simple. "God does not prevent the storms; he just helps us get through them." If I had not had this faith moving forward, I am not sure I would have survived the aftermath of the hurricane nor any of the other "storms" I have faced since then.

4. Life is not about learning the answers; it is more about asking the right questions.

In seventeen years of school, I spent a lot of time finding answers to questions. Not once can I remember receiving any training on asking the right questions. As a business owner, I assumed my job was to have all of the answers. When I didn't, I faked it until I could find the right answer.

It was not until I began my career as a consultant that I learned the beauty of asking questions. I have found that asking the right questions takes much more thought and can achieve much better results than just finding answers. My sons sometimes get very irritated with my practice of asking questions. They would rather I just give them answers. They are used to being spoon-fed in school with answers. What if we trained them to ask better questions instead?

A corollary to this life lesson is the following quote: "The more I learn, the less I know."

5. Life on the high road.

Early in my career I had a life mentor, Bob Jensen. He was a banker. One day in his office he shared a pearl of wisdom that has stayed with me ever since. He said that there were two roads in life; the high road and the low road. Any decision of significance would involve either taking the "high road" or the "low road." The "high road" was doing the right thing. Making choices that were good for me and for anyone else involved. The "low road" involved decisions that put either myself or other people at risk or danger.

Up to that point, I realized that I had taken the "low road" more times than I was comfortable admitting. In fact, I am not sure I actually gave much thought to the impact many of my decisions had on others. Since that time, I have tried very hard to stay on the "high road." I may have detoured on occasion, but I believe for the most part I have navigated my way much better on top.

6. Ninety percent of success in life is a product of just showing up.

I was not born with great intellect or any special skills. I was not blessed with speed of foot or mind. Therefore, through much of my life I have resorted to a learned skill in order to survive, and in some cases succeed: *just showing up.*

In school, I was one of those kids with nearly perfect attendance. I had to go to school. I could not afford to miss a day and try to make up work. The same applies to work. I may miss 1–2 days of work a year. I just can't afford to miss any more. I don't miss meetings. I don't miss appointments. I answer all phone calls when possible and, if not, I return all messages. I have to. I am just not smart enough to figure out which meetings to miss or which calls to avoid.

I am also not a big believer in blind luck. I truly believe that we make our luck. In fact, I believe that luck is a product of skill and opportunity. By not showing up, I leave skill by itself and… well, I am just not that good.

"The supreme accomplishment is to blur the line between work and play."

~ Arnold Toynbee

SEE IT, HIT IT

February 2009

Last week, nationally recognized speaker and best-selling author, Barbara Babbit Kaufman, spoke to one of my Vistage groups about "Attitude." Among her *"Ten Tips for Maintaining a Great Attitude"* was to create a personal mantra. A mantra is an abbreviated (3–5 words) personal mission statement. Kaufman suggested to my members that a personal mantra helps bring clarity and focus to our lives, and can help us maintain a great attitude.

During the course of Barbara's presentation I was reminded of my own journey toward creating a personal mantra, and the profound impact it has had on my life.

I have played tennis for most of my life. As a teenager I would play tennis after school as often as possible. I never took tennis lessons. I just enjoyed playing the game and competing against my friends. As an adult I have continued to play tennis as often as possible. I enjoy playing in tennis leagues such as USTA and ALTA, as well as playing recreational tennis with friends and neighbors. I dread the day that I will not be able to step onto the tennis court and compete at the highest level.

Several years ago my tennis game was as bad as it had ever been. I found myself getting increasingly frustrated about my game. I was losing more matches than I was winning. I was not enjoying the sport. I considered taking a tennis sabbatical. Not possible. I also considered taking tennis lessons. No time. Then I remembered a book that was given to me years ago titled *The Inner Game of Tennis*, written by Timothy Gallwey. This book single-handedly resurrected my tennis game.

My struggles in tennis at that time were very similar to those many athletes experience in a range of different sports. When I would hit a good tennis shot, I would think, "It's about time! Where's that shot been?" When I would hit a bad shot, I would mentally crucify myself, "Where did that shot come from? That was awful. You are a miserable tennis player." That inner discussion would go on until the next point. Imagine how excited I would be at that point to hit my next shot. The mental aspect of the game was killing me.

In his book, Dr. Gallwey discusses the importance of "quieting the mind" between points. Instead of analyzing each shot and trying to figure out what went wrong, just move on to the next point. I realized that I had most likely hit every possible shot on the tennis court hundreds, if not thousands, of times. I did not need to waste my time instructing myself how to hit each shot between points. Nothing constructive was coming out of this mental exercise.

I began to quiet my mind between points and focus on the task at hand. It was at this time that I developed a personal mantra for my tennis game: *See it, Hit it*. Before I would return serve, I pictured myself hitting the perfect return of service. Next, I would look for the tennis ball in the hand of the server as he prepared to serve. I would focus on nothing but that yellow, fuzzy ball as it left the server's hand, was struck by the tennis racket, and then approached my side of the net. I trusted my body to do what it had done quite competently thousands of times before... *See it, Hit it*. The results were fantastic! I began playing much better. I began winning more, and most importantly, I began to enjoy the game as I had for many years.

Not long after employing this new mental tool in my tennis game, I began to consider if this mantra would work as effectively outside of tennis. Is it possible that I could apply this tactic to my work?

I spend most of my time either in one-on-one or group meetings with clients and group members. It is not unusual in those meetings for me to have a conversation with the client while also having a conversation with myself: *Is this meeting going well? What could I be doing differently? What's the client thinking? Should I ask more questions? Did I spill something at lunch?*

Experiencing these dual conversations creates confusion, and certainly impacts my effectiveness as a listener and a consultant. I wonder what would be the impact of quieting my mind in these experiences? What if I could be more in the moment? It seemed that the same strategy that had changed my tennis game could also work there, too. I began to adopt my personal mantra, *See it, Hit it*, in my work and experienced very positive results. I could focus on the task at hand and not on what I thought was going on around me.

This is still a work in progress. I still find myself playing tennis and occasionally getting frustrated at missed shots. I can still lose my focus during the match and find myself replaying missed shots. I still have work to do here. Likewise, from time to time in my work I experience those fierce conversations with myself when I am trying to work with a client or group. Old habits are very hard to break.

What's your personal mantra? If you have a personal mission statement or core purpose, is it possible to narrow it down to a 3–5 word mantra? Life is increasingly complicated. I believe anything that helps us focus better and gain more clarity must be a good thing. In the meantime, you are welcome to borrow mine. *"See it, Hit it."*

*"Anything you vividly imagine,
ardently desire, sincerely believe
and enthusiastically act upon must,
absolutely must come to pass."*

~ SKIP BERTMAN, BASEBALL COACH

A Letter to My Son

July 2009

Leadership guru, Walter Wright, spoke to one of my Vistage CEO groups this past month. In consideration of our own management skills, he had each of us write a letter to someone we care deeply about who is about to begin his or her first management position. The letter is to bequeath the values I want this person to have on this initial leadership journey. Here is my letter:

Dear Taylor,

Congratulations on your new job as a manager! You have worked hard to achieve this position and I wish you great success. Based on my own leadership experience, here are the keys to your success:

- Be curious.

- Seek first to understand and then to be understood. (This comes from one of my favorite books, Steven Covey's *Seven Habits of Highly Effective People.*)

- Under-promise, over-deliver.

- Your people are watching you all the time. "It's show time."

- Be a great storyteller.

- Be humble.

- Be prepared to lead from the front and from behind.

- Hire people smarter and different than you.

- Fail often.

- Trust your instincts.

- Over-communicate.

- Laugh often.

- Be generous.

- Stay on the "high road."

Much love,

Dad

Writing this letter was a great learning exercise for me as it forced me to consider my most important leadership values. I encourage each of you to write a similar letter today even if you have no one to send it to right away. Write it, put it in an envelope, and wait for the right opportunity to share it with someone you care deeply about.

*"When the student is ready,
the teacher appears."*

~ Zen Buddhist maxim

ARE YOU READY FOR THE RECOVERY?

February 2010

"Now is the time to act."

This quote comes from the January edition of the newsletter, *EcoTrends*, written by two of the country's leading economists, Alan and Brian Beaulieu (http://ecotrends.org). They very accurately predicted the recent collapse of the economy and the recession that followed. Now they have set their sights on the recovery.

Imagine a series of bell curves representing the ups and downs of our economy. According to most economists, including the Beaulieus, the economy has moved just past the bottom of the curve. We have experienced the worst of the recession. For many small business owners I know it doesn't feel much better. There are not a lot of Mardi Gras-like celebrations in the streets.

However, the key is to acknowledge that the recovery has started, and ask yourself what action you need to take in your business as a result of this upward swing in the economy. Here are several possibilities for small business owners:

• **A key hire.** You may have been holding off on making an important hiring decision. Now is the time to move forward. It's certainly a buyer's market for talent today. Maybe it's a star sales person or a key manager.

• **Acquire market share.** It will still be difficult for many small businesses to grow revenue this year. However, now is the time to grow your share of the customer pie. Add clients. Take away customers from your competitors. Possibly acquire a competitor. Find a strategic partner. Imagine a "land grab" of sorts. Claim your territory.

- **Expansion.** This might include a new product or service, moving into a new geographic region, or expanding your production capacity with new technology or equipment.

As I look at this list there seems to be one very important resource missing that is required before a business can take action—**cash.** Hopefully in the past eighteen months you have been hoarding cash in preparation for this time. If not, it is imperative that you find cash now. While there is certainly credit cash today in the economy, I also know that there is credit available for small businesses. There are banks lending money. I have had a number of my members successfully acquire lines of credit or extend their lines in the past six months. You need cash to act.

In this regard I am reminded of a quote from economist Brian Beaulieu: "Most companies that go bankrupt do so during an upturn in the economy… they don't have and can't get the *working capital* necessary to compete."

I am also reminded of a fact I heard recently about small business failure. The speaker was a world-famous mountain climber. He had climbed the tallest peaks in the world. He shared great stories of his expeditions. He also spoke of climbing failures. He shared with the audience that more mountaineers die going down the side of one of these treacherous peaks than going up. Imagine that. Imagine how hard it is to get to the top of a Mount Everest or Mount Kilimanjaro. More die returning to base than making the amazing climb to the top. When asked why, the speaker responded with one word: *fatigue.*

I am certain this is true for small businesses as well. More business will fail over the next twelve months than did the past twelve months. Why? There are two reasons. First, they need cash, as described by Mr. Beaulieu. Second is fatigue, as described by the mountain climbing expert. I find this to be very prevalent today with many of my Vistage members and clients. They are exhausted. This has been a very tough "climb" the past year and a half. I am tired as well. I need a break, yet I must remind myself that…

"Now is the time to act."

"The significant problems we are facing cannot be solved at the same level of thinking we were at when we created them."

~ Albert Einstein

IT'S THE SEASON OF THANKSGIVING

This time of year I am prone to reflect on the gifts of life for which I am most thankful. I hope that by sharing my list with you, you might do the same with your own list, with those for whom you care the most.

I am thankful for the clients I work with who challenge me in ways they may never realize and in turn provide me with rewards beyond my own belief.

I am thankful for the chill of fall, the warmth of spring, and the brilliant colors of both seasons.

I am thankful for low interest rates, relatively high employment, and an economics degree that helps me make some sense of both.

I am thankful to have a mom still living who inspires me with her tremendous spirit and passion for life, and a dad who left this world way before his time, but who lives with me each moment of the day.

I am thankful that almost every day my computer turns on and works flawlessly despite the bombardment of spam, spyware, and nasty viruses.

I am thankful that I live in a country where my religious faith is used less as a sword and more as a shield.

I am thankful for the great entrepreneurs of our time, such as Ray Kroc, Jack Welch, Bill Gates, and Herb Kelleher, who have, through their own classic and magnificent examples, paved the way for the entrepreneurs of the future.

I am thankful for having relatively good health that allows me to run, swim, play tennis, and barely keep up with two rambunctious teenage boys.

I am thankful that despite all of the complexities of business today, despite the overwhelming assortment of technologies we are plagued by, despite the ever-increasing number of adverse events we as business owners face each day, the basic principles of business have remained steadfast. It's still all about solving the customer's problems profitably.

I am thankful that at the age of eighteen I followed my instincts and traveled a great distance to pursue my post-secondary education. This decision resulted in a great academic experience, a band of lifetime friends, and the opportunity to meet the girl of my dreams and my life partner for 22 years.

Lastly, I am quite thankful that **Small Business *still* Matters**.

Have a very Happy Thanksgiving.

"There is more to life than increasing its speed."

~ MAHATMA GANDHI

I am From

October 2010

Last year I had each of my Vistage members write a poem about themselves. Here is mine.

I am from Oklahoma and Missouri. Colorado and Michigan. Parents Dorothy and Robert instilled upon me solid mid-western values such as honesty and respect. Humility and integrity.

I am from Miami, Florida growing up barefoot, tanned, and sand between my toes. I experienced an undefeated Dolphin season, a Cuban invasion, and a hurricane named Andrew.

I am from New Orleans where I attended college at Tulane, learned brotherhood in a fraternity, and studied nightlife in the French Quarter.

I am from Atlanta. Married to my college sweetheart Remy for 28 years. Proudly raised two boys, Taylor and Carter. Built a consulting practice to CEOs.

I live in a world where my religion is private and my politics are public. My music is loud and my voice is soft. I like big pets and small cars. Vacations at the beach and retreats in the mountains. Short books and long walks. Spicy food and mild weather.

My life journey speeds along a two-lane country highway. Lots of stops. Interesting people. Lessons learned. Always navigating the high road.

Notes: